Take Off Your Shoes

Take Off Your Shoes

One Man's Journey from the Boardroom to Bali and Back

Ben Feder

Radius Book Group
New York

Distributed by Radius Book Group
A Division of Diversion Publishing Corp.
443 Park Avenue South, Suite 1008
New York, NY 10016
www.RadiusBookGroup.com

First edition: April 2018
Hardcover ISBN: 978-1-63576-367-6
Trade Paperback ISBN: 978-1-63576-495-6
eBook ISBN: 978-1-63576-368-3

Quote from David Whyte, printed with permission from Many Rivers Press,
www.davidwhyte.com. David Whyte, "Fire in the Earth," *Fire in the Earth*,
together with ©Many Rivers Press, Langley, WA USA.

A portion of the proceeds from the sale of this book will be donated to *Save a Child's Heart*. The results of their work are a testament to the power of compassion.

To Victoria, Live, Love, Laugh
and
To my late father,
whose boundless legacy
needs no words

And we know, when Moses was told,
in the way he was told,
"Take off your shoes!" He grew pale from that simple

reminder of fire in the dusty earth.
He never recovered
his complicated way of loving again

and was free to love in the same way
he felt the fire licking at his heels loved him.

—David Whyte, "Fire in the Earth"

introduction

I wrote this book for my children. I wanted them to understand my motivations for walking away from a lucrative and engaging career and all but burning my bridges. I wanted to leave them a memento that went beyond the photo album or the family blog we kept during the break. They may not understand or have an interest in it now, but when they are in their twenties and thirties, when many men and women start asking questions about their parents, I believe the book will be helpful to them. If my children find it enlightening, it will have achieved its aim. If others learn something from it, that is also good.

The other reason I wrote this book is that many of the people I met who inquired about the trip asked me to write it. They thought it was an important story to tell. For some, the story stoked fantasies about what it would be like to take time off. For others, it enabled them to live vicariously through our experiences. Still others thought about making concrete plans. But everybody wanted to know about it.

One of the things that led me to take a sabbatical was my increasing curiosity about brain plasticity and our ability to deliberately cultivate a sense of well-being. I read extensively on the subject and did my own research. In this book, I have tried to weave in what I learned through the academic and popular writing about our ability to change our lives by changing our minds. I applied that learning to my own actions and experiences. I have also tried to sprinkle in some of what I have learned about leadership along the way.

Trying something new and creative, without regard to success or failure, was another reason to write the book and in a way is what it's about. When I started to write it, I had a preconceived notion of what the exercise would be. I imagined banging away at my keyboard, the words flowing through my mind faster than my fingers could type them. In fact, the process was much slower and more methodical. Sometimes the words did not come at all. I persevered, and this is the result.

One of my friends from Bali, Renee Martyna, researched the cohort of professionals that I had inadvertently joined and whom she called *knowmads*: knowledge professionals like me who had stepped off the career track to pursue an unexplained need to be a vagabond. Taken together, she thought, they told a universal narrative even though each individual story was highly personal. She found that the one factor that separated those who could adjust back to regular life after sabbatical and those who could not was their ability to tell their own story.

I tend to be skeptical of authors who claim they write for the benefit of others. But it was my son Oliver, pushing me to write, who said in his preteenage years, "I think other people can really learn from what you did."

one 𝒲

On a cool spring Wednesday morning, in the Meat-packing District of Lower Manhattan, black Cadillac Escalades ferrying executives from across town pulled up to the entrance of the W Hotel. Abundant clouds dampened the light but posed no threat. A news van parked outside raised its antenna to full height. Inside the hotel lobby, a CNBC reporting team was ensconced. Two floors down, in a windowless basement meeting room, management and shareholders of Take-Two Interactive, a multinational video game publisher, assembled for an unusual gathering. Regulators required the company to hold the meeting annually, but it had been eighteen months since the previous one—so late that Take-Two was in danger of losing its listing on the NASDAQ stock exchange.

Shareholders arriving at this meeting were deeply unhappy with the state of the company. Take-Two had been under investigation by the Securities and Exchange Commission (SEC), the Federal Trade Commission, and the Manhattan District Attorney's Office. There were financial irregularities, and the company's auditors had not certified its annual report. A former CEO was ultimately indicted and pled guilty to falsifying business records, and the board of directors was fractious.

Not only had many investors shied away from buying the company's stock, but it was one of the most shorted stocks on the NASDAQ. Short sellers, who sell stock first and buy it later, gambled on the company's stock price declining even further. Some investors bet that Take-Two would continue to circle the drain; others bet on a rosier outlook, hoping that a larger competitor might gobble it up. One way or another, in the eyes of many, the demise of the company's independence was imminent.

Ordinarily, shareholder meetings like this were perfunctory, and unless something controversial was on the agenda, votes were cast by the shareholders well in advance of the meeting, usually in support of the resolutions proposed by management. This time was different. Shareholders representing most of the votes were present to voice and act on their displeasure. They had no intention of voting for the management's resolutions.

They were there because my partners and I had arranged for them to be there. We were betting that the company would succeed. We thought it owned strong assets, especially the monster hit video game *Grand Theft Auto*. Take-Two was also about to release a promising new game, *BioShock*, and had a leading NBA basketball game franchise.

Back in high school, I was an entrepreneurial kid, scheming up ways to make extra cash while my friends were playing ball. As I matured, I meandered through a liberal arts education, searching for a professional calling. I had been a research analyst after college and attended business school because commerce seemed to be in my blood.

But it wasn't until my first real job working in business development at Rupert Murdoch's News Corporation that I developed an ambition to become the kind of businessman that he was, to cleverly build new businesses or buy existing ones. I had founded and grown a start-up that I was proud of. I sold it but still harbored ambitions of leading a much larger enterprise. When I found like-minded partners, we started a firm with the ambition to build a diversified media company through acquisitions. Since we had no money, we were forced to fight our way into tough situations. We were entrepreneurial because we had to be. We were hungry, ambitious, and aggressive.

Partnering with private equity investors, we took on highly troubled situations that we could fix and turn around. Using that model, we had successfully gained control of a number of small- and medium-sized companies. And we delivered good results. But nothing was as large or creative as Take-Two. Nothing exhibited its enormous potential, which, because its games were so highly regarded, projected a market presence that was vastly larger than its actual size.

The situation was unusual for us because the company was publicly traded. Since no single shareholder owned enough company stock to control the organization, there was no single owner with whom we could work. If one shareholder sought to coordinate with another, they needed to abide by a complex set of regulations stipulated by the SEC and corporate case law in Delaware, where the company was incorporated. If we were to be successful in effecting change, we needed to be clever and creative. And we needed to be careful to stay strictly within the regulations. Inadvertently tripping over a regulatory wire, even a small one, would be fatal to our plans and our careers.

My partners were initially skeptical. Take-Two was in deep trouble. Putting my credibility on the line and convinced that the company's unresolved legal issues were old news, I took a contrarian view. Any investor who cared already knew about the problems, and if the company was not inclined to fix them itself, the government agencies that had been investigating would force the issue. It seemed unlikely that there were any horrors still to be discovered—the bad news was in the past. In the argot of Wall Street, it was all "priced in"—the current valuation already took all the rot into account. To Strauss, the senior partner at the firm I cofounded, I likened the company to an open, pus-oozing wound: it looked disgusting, but pus is a sign of a healing infection. My other partners reluctantly came on board. We needed to win.

For about six months, my team and I had worked with the best lawyers in the business to garner support for our plan to change the composition of the board and senior management of Take-Two. We worked with some of the smartest fund managers and some of the largest pools of money in the investment community to navigate a path through the labyrinth of legal obstacles despite periodically running down legal blind alleys.

When the company announced a snap shareholder meeting to be held almost immediately, we sprang. We coordinated a group of shareholders to file with the SEC and disclosed our intention: the shareholders would attend the meeting—in person—and would nominate a slate of directors to the board as a direct challenge to the one proposed by the company. If that board was successfully elected, the shareholders intended to oust the CEO and, potentially, the CFO.

A vote of this sort from the floor of a shareholder meeting was rare in the extreme. Effecting a management change in precisely this form, we were told, had never before occurred in American corporate history. Ordinarily, a change of this sort would involve a proxy fight, in which nominees to the board are announced well ahead of time by activist shareholders, and a campaign to garner voting proxies would ensue. Proxy fights over one or two directors are often the source of a bitter contest between the company's management and its shareholders. In this case, we proposed to change out not just a few directors but five out of seven. That would leave only two incumbent directors, resulting in a wholesale change in the ranks of senior management. Although we carefully designed the action to minimize disruption, there was no mistaking our intent. It was a hostile take-over.

∽

The meeting room at the hotel was packed. Two concrete floors separated the basement from ground level and obstructed connections to wireless networks. The professionals in the room were cut off from their advisers, partners, and in my case, my wife, Victoria, who was waiting anxiously for news. Once our opponents and we descended into that chamber, there was no communication with the outside world until the battle was over.

Strauss and I took seats in the front row. I twisted around to look behind me. The room was packed with white men in ties speaking in hushed tones. I swung back to face the front. A tall man paced near the dais. He had his white hair slicked back and wore a three-piece, pinstriped Italian suit, starched white shirt, and red tie. I leaned toward Strauss. "This guy is obviously paid too much." I was thinking about the potential cost-cutting exercise ahead of us and blithely assumed that Daddy Warbucks worked for the company. Strauss smiled calmly.

The success or failure of our efforts would come down to a simple raise of hands. Normally, with shareholders casting votes in advance, tumbleweed could roll through the empty rooms of annual meetings populated often by retirees who owned a few shares or shareholders who wished to push a pet cause. This time, shareholders needed to be physically present in order to nominate a board in the manner that we were proposing—from the floor. Representatives from major hedge funds and mutual funds who had arrived specifically to support our bid for change gathered in the narrow room. A portfolio manager from one firm flew in from Italy for the sole purpose of casting his vote.

Officers of the company sat at a dais facing a long column of narrow rows of seats. An empty podium stood lonely to the side. At the start of the meeting, the general counsel of the company rose to the podium to open the proceedings. The room fell silent. He introduced the company's nominees for the board of directors. "Are there any other nominations for the board of directors?" he asked the shareholders sitting in the audience.

Emmanuel Ferreira, representing the largest shareholder, rose to his feet. He cleared his throat and stated his name and the number of shares he represented. "I'd like to nominate the following directors." He then listed a full slate of directors to the board, only two of whom were not new. I was nominated along with Strauss and three other independent directors.

Months of planning had led to this showdown. Fueled by adrenaline and a deep competitive drive, we had fought and clawed. Now, although we knew that any outcome was possible, we were confident.

After Ferreira read his list of nominees, a vote was called. I looked around the room to see hands shoot in the air in favor of our slate. Auditors walked around the room to collect forms. It took them more than an hour to count and authenticate the votes. The general counsel pulled us aside. "It looks like you're the clear winners." I felt the surge of victory well up inside me, that familiar sense of hard-fought achievement that I craved like an addict. "Congratulations," he said. "I'll see you in the office in the morning."

In that brief moment, the company turned over its management. It had a brand-new set of directors and a new management team. Strauss became chairman, and my colleague Karl became an executive vice president. I became CEO.

I imagined for a moment what the next day in the office would be like. We had just fired the CEO, and others in the company surely expected more dismissals would follow. I felt a twinge of discomfort. My mother was a psychotherapist, and I grew up with an appreciation of and curiosity about the inner lives of others. I felt both power and empathy, and in that flash, also confusion. Success was rarely unbridled. I willed away any sentimentality. If you have a hammer, use it.

I was at the helm of a two-thousand-person organization about whose inner workings I knew precious little. What I did know was how to successfully reengineer a company's internal operations in order to grow and create greater profits. And I knew how to position a company within its industry.

My firm's explicit intention was for me to serve for a short period while we launched a search for a full-time leader. I expected to head the company for six months, but the board asked me to stay. The gig lasted nearly four years.

two

I arrived home late for dinner one night. Oliver and Rita, our two middle children, ran down the hall in a race to be the first to hug me, but before they reached me, Oliver checked Rita into the wall. She was unhurt but started to scream. Their combative relationship was starting to grate on me. Dinner was already under way, and as I walked toward the table, Victoria shot me a glance that I recognized all too well. Our son Sam, the oldest of our four children, was staring at his plate, his hands over his ears to block out the noise of his siblings. I joined the mostly raucous dinner, the conversation half-comprehensible as children vied for attention, the food half-eaten, Sam half-present.

After dinner, in one of our increasingly heated behind-the-bedroom-door discussions, Victoria lost patience. "I never signed up for this!" My tenure at Take-Two had gone from being short term to permanent. My schedule had filled with dinners, breakfasts, and travel, and the rising tension between us was aggravated by Victoria's own growing commitments. She managed not only our four children's overscheduled lives but also a thriving community center and preschool that she had founded and in which she had been deeply engaged for seven years.

Our conversations were becoming increasingly transactional, dealing with the logistics of our lives but sharing little of each other's inner selves. I simply was not engaged in our family. Even when I was physically present, I was distracted. A constant flow of emails from multiple time zones competed intensely for my attention. She felt abandoned, we were growing apart, and I felt helpless to stop it or reverse the trend.

"I can't control my schedule," I said to her. "I did actually sign up for this, and I want to see it through. I want to succeed."

"When was the last time you were home on time for dinner? Do you think our kids don't notice you're never around? Do you think they don't notice you on a conference call when you're supposedly watching their ball game?" Of course she was right. I committed to being home for dinner more, even though I suspected it was only a stopgap.

I returned from work one evening to find Sam sequestered as usual in his room doing homework. I cracked open his bedroom door and poked my head in. "Hey, Sam." He barely looked up from his math problems and returned a teenage grunt.

Victoria called the kids to dinner. Nobody came. It took a few more calls for the other three kids to finally arrive in age order: first Oliver, then Rita and Nava. Only a final, angry summons convinced Sam to shuffle out from the barricade of his bedroom.

Victoria was in the kitchen spooning rice from the cooker onto a serving platter. I asked my kids, "Did anything strange or wonderful happen today?" Nava, in kindergarten, came up with a story, but Sam was lost in his thoughts.

When Victoria joined us, Sam grunted, "Chicken." I assumed he wanted someone to pass him the chicken.

"A verb, Sam," Victoria said. "We need a verb."

I knew Sam was going through a normal teenage phase, but still I felt my frustration rise. I lectured him to take responsibility for his family relationships but was saddened by my perceived loss of our father-son connection. When dinner ended and Victoria and I were washing up, I turned to her and said, "Four more years of this and he's out of the house and off to college.

It's nonstop work in his high school, and it's nonstop work for me. By the time he's gone, instead of building a relationship with him, I'll have spent years building a company for some promise of a reward that seems always to be receding into the future."

Victoria saw the situation similarly. "It's not just Sam. Your relationship with your other kids is suffering too. Especially Nava."

Nava was an avid reader even at a young age. On weekends, she had no time for or interest in me. When I wanted to play with her, she glared at me and then stuck her nose in her book. Between her being lost in her thoughts and my responding to the demands of my job, I was missing her childhood.

Rita, nine, was in a tough, catty, preteen social environment that deeply pained her. Nothing extreme ever happened; it could be as subtle as an eye roll or as blatant as a rejection at the lunch table. But Rita tended to process feelings on a deeper level than most. She often returned from school tearful or belligerent before she revealed what had happened that day. She was being emotionally bullied and needed my help.

I was less concerned about my relationship with Oliver. He had a tight group of friends, twelve-year-old boys who had been together since kindergarten. He was past his formative years by the time I started at Take-Two but not so old that I feared that, like Sam, his departure from home was imminent.

Still, my day-to-day experiences had gradually diverged from those of my family. We were no longer leading the same lives. When I came home with stories of travel, new cultures, or discussions with men and women who were highly effective in the world, my family was increasingly uninterested. And I sensed it acutely.

∿

One evening, I returned home late. Exhausted from the day, I sank down into our red sofa and rested my feet on the coffee table. The younger kids were already asleep. Victoria came into the room and closed the door. She had just returned from a weekend retreat with women working in business and philanthropy. One of them had recently spent a year in Barcelona. Victoria had been gripped by the thought of it and spent the entire weekend peppering her friend with questions and squeezing out of her every bit of advice and information that she could. I listened to Victoria talk about her friend traveling abroad with her family. It was something Victoria and I had fantasized about on and off throughout our marriage.

Victoria fell silent, grabbed my hand, and gave me a piercing look. "Let's go." She then used a word I had thought was reserved for academics and librarians: "Let's take a *sabbatical*."

Dog-tired, I immediately focused on the negative impact a sabbatical could have on the career I'd worked so hard to develop. But I took a beat and considered the possibility. Having poured so much of myself into getting where I was, the thought of suddenly pulling myself out of the game terrified me. We talked more about how we could make the money work and deal with the kids' schooling.

I reflected on my time at Take-Two. We had achieved great initial success. We had taken the company from death's door to one of the best positions in the industry. None of it was easy. No organization hums along perfectly, firing on all cylinders all the time. Each is thorny in its own way, and working through those organizational challenges was part of the fun of leadership. But it was intense work for a long time, and it took its toll.

Now, as Victoria knew, battle fatigue was setting in, and somehow I couldn't shake it. In the past, my cure for exhaustion had never been rest but rededication. I would recommit to the cause and lean into the machine. Lately, though, when I dug deep for that commitment, I was coming up empty.

The caffeine that fueled my days and the wine that buoyed my evenings also interrupted my sleep, and insomnia was becoming chronic. I could not help feeling the emotional and physical costs of personal sacrifices made for the greater good, for the mission on which I was so focused and in which I so believed. I was getting tired of the endless striving, the ambition, and the desire for more. More wanting seemed to lead only to more wanting. I wondered if I could simply declare victory and move on.

"I need some time," I said to Victoria.

∿

Over the years, I learned that complex decisions, which required me to simultaneously consider many variables, were better made after they marinated in the back of my mind rather than being dealt with directly, rationally, and immediately.

I was not alone. In one experiment, researchers provided participant groups complex and detailed information about four different apartments and asked them to choose the best one. The groups were allowed to devote varying amounts of time and attention to the problem. One group in particular had their conscious thoughts deliberately diverted by engaging in a task, like playing anagrams, designed for that purpose. That group performed better than undistracted groups, regardless of the amount of time the other groups had to consider the problem. In other words, often the best way to resolve complex situations is to find a distraction, something else to focus on. While it may not feel like it, the gears of the problem-solving mind crank away in the background even while the conscious mind is focused elsewhere. There was even evidence suggesting that attempts to verbalize or otherwise articulate the reasons we make decisions can lead to biases and poor decision-making.

I emailed Gloria, an executive coach I knew, and invited her to my Greenwich Village office for a few sessions. I needed a confidential sounding board to check my sanity.

"If I took a sabbatical, would I destroy my career?"

Gloria sat across my blond pinewood desk. Nine-foot-tall windows were at my back and an exposed redbrick wall at my right. The radiator banged and hissed as if to punctuate our conversation. The furniture layout was a throwback to an old-school style of management: with me behind the desk in a high-backed chair and whomever I was talking to sitting across from me in one of two low-slung chairs, the design made it clear who the boss was.

"I've coached lots of senior executives and have seen a lot of management situations." Gloria was at least twenty years my senior. "I know you have a lot at stake here. It's true that the career risks are high. But to use a worn-out phrase, are you living to work or working to live?"

I sensed she understood that something about my situation was different from her usual assignments. Executives often engaged coaches when they wanted to grow or change or when they understood they were getting in their own way as they pushed to advance their careers.

"I've advised some terrific executives," she said, "guys who go from one great job to an even better one. They're constantly achieving and rising. Do you know what happens to those people?"

"Tell me."

"They drop dead of a heart attack at fifty-five."

That hit me. My own father suffered that fate at sixty-one. I was determined not to let it happen to me or to my children as long as I could help it. It was one of the main reasons I exercised like crazy and did everything I could to manage my risk factors.

I'd recently seen my doctor for a physical checkup. "What's with this?" She poked my midsection, where stress-related weight gain typically appears in men. My blood pressure, which had always been low, was approaching levels that indicated hypertension. While speaking to my doctor, I thought of Bob, a friend I had lost to cancer at the age of forty-five. Who knew when this was all going to end?

I said to Gloria, "The board is really going to be pissed off."

"The board is going to do what the board's going to do. You need to do this for you. You need to work up the courage."

If I were to leave, lots of people with a stake in my decision—my partners, board directors, and key employees—were not going to be happy with me. Gloria encouraged me to see past pleasing them. She asked me to find the confidence that there would be a career after a sabbatical.

"We tend to live our lives conditionally," she said. "When such and such happens, then I'll do this or that. But the conditions are never quite right. Maybe when we're dead, everything will fall into place. But why wait for the situation to ripen to perfection? Why not act now?"

I added it up. Taking sabbatical would require significant sacrifice. It would mean giving up a leadership position in a high-profile company, forfeiting material compensation, and potentially separating from a business partnership that had been supportive and meaningful to me. It could even mean separating from my business partner, Strauss, who had been a mentor for many years and someone with whom I felt I could accomplish great things.

Recently, though, our relationship had become tense and fraught for reasons I couldn't quite explain. Perhaps it was like the moment when a marriage becomes untenable—the parties involved don't know why; they simply know the magic is gone. I knew in the depths of my being, in the way that one simply knows something to be true, that I needed to shake things up. And yet I was ambivalent. I wanted in the worst way for it to work.

Then one day on my walk home, I glanced up at another man, about my age, walking toward me. He, like me, was well dressed and obviously had a career that paid well and probably a family at home in an affluent neighborhood like mine. Our eyes met for a moment. He looked tense, exhausted, and distracted, and he seemed detached from the conversation he was having on his phone. My doppelgänger trudged past, out of sight, a mere blip in my day, but at that moment, I froze. I felt I could not take another step.

This is where it happens. Where husbands and fathers turn into men they never intended to be. They follow their ambitions, their careers, and their deluded views of what it means to succeed. Somewhere along the way, these well-meaning family men and woman eventually realize that they have neglected key relationships that feed them, relationships that are critical to their well-being. And if that realization comes late in their lives, the time may have passed to do anything about it. Children will have grown, and much water will have flowed under the bridge of their spousal relationships. If I didn't choose the path, the path would choose me.

On a Sunday morning, when Victoria and I lingered over breakfast tea, I said, "I'm in."

"Really?"

"Truly."

"Really, really?"

"Truly, truly."

As the words came out of my mouth, I had some lingering doubt but didn't express it. When it came to decision-making, I had learned that second-guessing was a paralyzing affliction. Besides, I knew how Victoria hated when I equivocated. I committed. We committed. And when we did, we felt a soaring elation. We were set free by the sheer imagining of what we were about to do. We basked in the weightlessness of our decision. When doubts plagued me, I did not waver. If I needed to leave something behind at work to make this sabbatical happen, it was probably time to go anyway. I felt that initial commitment as pure liberty.

A few nights later, I turned to Victoria. "So. Where do you want to go?"

Meanwhile, it had occurred to me that I was not the only one who needed a change. In the aftermath of 9/11, Victoria had heard a calling to build a Jewish community in our neighborhood. We lived only ten blocks from Ground Zero, and Victoria was struck by the lack of support from the larger Jewish community. The church groups were out in droves, but the Jewish community was unfocused, unorganized, and, frankly, absent.

Victoria founded a group called Jewish Community Project (JCP), whose mission was to create a modern community life that was rich in values, culture, and tradition for the families and individuals living in Lower Manhattan. The purpose of JCP was to create a network of support that would be available to families in good times and in more challenging situations, such as the aftermath of 9/11. It started in our living room but grew to become one of the city's prominent preschool programs and adult education learning centers. She had achieved what she had set out to do, working not only as president of the board but also, at times, as de facto executive director. For the rest of the board, this was a happy situation: a competent, committed, full-time, volunteer CEO. They hoped and perhaps assumed she would stay on forever. But Victoria needed a break and was ready for a change.

Victoria, like me, was achievement oriented, and we saw our kids setting off on the same path. They went to a Jewish prep school in Manhattan. They focused so relentlessly on their grades and competed so hard through academic achievement that we instituted a family prohibition against sharing grades at the dinner table. Sam especially was deeply vested in his own success at school. He was doing well and had a personality that chased incentives. Put a piece of cheese at the end of the labyrinth and he'd find his way through to it. Every pat on the back for academic performance was encouragement for him to achieve more. Victoria and I began to realize that a product of all that so-called achievement was a craving for yet more achievement and more success, a constant feeding that knew no end. We knew that while achievement contributed to a sense of well-being, there had to be something more. It was possibly driving out a lighter, fun-oriented part of his personality. We needed him to realize there is more to be gained from a well-rounded approach to studies, athletics, and life in general.

Victoria and I had a growing sense that we were stuck in a mindless trap, trying to achieve goals that were somehow external to ourselves: advancing our careers, making more than we needed, eyeing New York apartments that were bigger or nicer than ours even though ours was perfectly sufficient and, we thought, beautiful. Striving for those external goals came at the expense of relationships, family, and time to reflect. What happened to the fantasy we had when we were younger of traveling together as a family? I was tunneling headlong into the job, deeper and deeper, feeding my burning desire to succeed. It was only in moments of rare clarity that I thought I had arrived at a crossroads.

We had no sabbatical destination in mind, but the entire planet was open to us. She pulled up an extra chair, and we sat side by side looking at our computer monitor, the suspended orb of Google Earth slowly spinning on the screen. With a click of the mouse, we flew around the world as if on a magic carpet, ferreting out nooks of the globe that held promise. We checked out Catalonia's Costa Brava and Brazil's tech hub and party island city, Florianópolis. We scrolled southeast to the Lake District in Chile, then north to the rainforests and coasts of Costa Rica and Mexico's artist town, San Miguel de Allende. We rotated the virtual earth to Hangzhou in China, a picturesque city south of Shanghai, and numerous destinations in the vast regions of Asia. But no destination seemed to jump from the screen as the obvious right one.

Over the next few weeks, we kept returning to the internet, searching now not for the ultimate answer but for information that would help us decide. We sought out families that had gone on sabbatical and read their blogs. Some had traveled around the globe as vagabonds; others stayed in one location. Some had taken a full year, others only a few months. Some spent their time in a developing country, others in Europe.

At one point we considered staying in perpetual motion and traveling around the world for a year. Victoria put together an itinerary: start in Africa, work our way through the south of India, then on to Cambodia, and from there to Bali, Indonesia, to spend our Passover holiday. From there we would travel north to Vietnam, China, and Japan. I thought the whole affair sounded exhausting, especially since constant travel was something from which I was trying to escape. And it would mean homeschooling our children, something that appealed in theory but, I knew, would fall apart in practice.

Despite the promise held by the enormously expansive prospect of taking off for an extended period, we were coming up empty. Bouncing around was not a good way to go about things. A lesson from my college rowing days sprang to mind. Navigating in a long shell is difficult. Coxswains steer straight by using a point: an object directly ahead of the boat at which to aim to keep the boat going in a straight line. We needed a focal point.

"We need to start with goals or we're never going to get anywhere," Victoria said. Earlier in her career, she had been a management consultant and now brought her discipline to bear. She pulled out a yellow legal pad and pen. We batted around ideas of what we wanted from our time away. When we were done, we looked at the page filled with circles, exclamation points, and underlining.

"Let's take a step back," she said. "The thing we want most is to experience something new and exciting together as a family, right?" She tapped the sheet in front of us. "All of these are secondary."

True. I wanted us to reconnect with each other and develop bonds while the kids were still young. I had traveled around the world and experienced so much on my own. I was keenly aware that as sophisticated as New York kids can be, Manhattan could also be the beginning, middle, and end of their life experience. Underlying all our goals was the desire for our children to experience a part of the world that was vastly different from their own, to challenge their senses and identities. We wanted to expose them to diversity, not just in the American sense of the word, but also in the planetary meaning.

Still, we needed to winnow down the choices. We looked again at the sheet. We wanted to skip winter on sabbatical and avoid the cold for one season. We needed a school that could support our children in English even as they learned a new language and experienced a foreign culture. Our destination needed to be central enough to allow us to travel regionally without too much hassle—New Zealand, for all its beauty, was out. Easy access to the outdoors was critical; we lived in a large city, and as exciting as a foreign city could be, cycling and hiking were priorities. We agreed to avoid big cities even though that would make it more difficult to find a suitable school for the kids.

Our travel needed to be affordable. We easily eliminated many destinations in Europe and Japan as too expensive. The whole affair was going to be funded by renting our New York apartment for what seemed to us to be crazy-high rates. And we needed to be far away. After reading in *A Year in Provence* about a couple who moved from England to France for one year and spent their first six months hosting their friends and family who popped by to visit, we knew that if we were truly to get away, we needed to create some distance between ourselves and our lives at home.

Our family observed many of our Jewish traditions and practices. New York City, home to a vast Jewish population, did not challenge our children's identities any more than it challenged Victoria's, born and raised in that liberal-tending city. Our children lived in a bubble and rarely felt like outsiders. They went to a Jewish school, had mostly Jewish friends, and were educated along Jewish themes.

Victoria and I didn't regret the way our kids were growing up. We had deliberately set it up that way. We aimed to imbue our children with a strong sense of heritage. But we recognized too the limitations of that goal if our children were to be thoughtful and full participants in the world in which they lived. We knew they could only benefit from leaving New York and experiencing the world, even if that meant challenging their sense of self. We knew too that finding a middle path of holding on to identity on the one hand while challenging it on the other was a difficult trick.

Reviewing all these goals and comparing them to the information we gathered, a single destination had poked through our filters.

〜

I emailed Strauss and asked to meet in a week or two, whenever he had time on his schedule. He shot back within minutes: "How's tomorrow morning at eight? I'll come downtown." We arranged for coffee at Le Pain Quotidien in Tribeca.

Strauss and I had worked so closely together for nearly two decades that we could finish each other's sentences. We didn't waste a lot of time with pleasantries. "What's on your mind?" he asked as we sat at a rustic wooden table.

I was nervous. At various times, Strauss had been my mentor, partner, or boss—lately, all three simultaneously. He meant a great deal to me. I cared deeply about what he thought, about both the sabbatical idea and how his view of me might shift. For all I knew, he might want to change things too. I knew I needed a break but desperately wanted to preserve our relationship and what I could of our partnership.

I had a sense of how this conversation might go. I thought I'd be able to pursue my plans to take a break and still leave the door open to returning to the firm. But I was prepared for other possibilities too, including Strauss insisting that I choose between staying with the firm and leaving for good. That would have terminated our partnership permanently.

"I've done everything the board has asked me to do," I said. "The turnaround is in hand; the company is in great shape and well positioned to grow. But I want to give you a lot of lead time about something I intend to do, something I need to do."

He picked at a callus just below his left ring finger, the inevitable result of disciplined weight training.

"I owe my family some time. I'm going to take a sabbatical."

Strauss shifted in his chair and slouched slightly. "How long do you intend to be away?"

"Six to twelve months." I was flexible on the timing. A full year seemed like an awfully long time.

I half hoped that he would try to convince me to stay or at least to gain some understanding of what was going on. He seemed upset by what I was saying but didn't ask for an explanation. His quick mind was already navigating a path forward. He offered his support. We talked about an economic arrangement. It was unlikely that I could return to the helm of Take-Two, but we would try to persuade the board. If I chose to return to the partnership, the door was open. If not, there would be economic consequences. It took about two more minutes to hammer out some remaining details, but in the end, the conversation was straightforward and unemotional. I thought the arrangement was fair, even generous. I wondered if others who had a stake in the outcome, including the board of directors, would think so too.

Then Strauss said, "Whatever's happening at home, as far as I'm concerned, it's not too late to change your mind." He didn't want me to go, and there was a limit to his patience. I looked into his eyes but could read nothing more. I flashed to the moment when I committed to Victoria and held firm now as I did then. There was no turning back.

three 𝔷

Victoria and I met Sam for lunch at Kitchenette, a diner on Chambers Street in Tribeca. At fourteen, Sam was one year away from entering his freshman year at the Ramaz School on the Upper East Side. Victoria's friend who went on sabbatical in Barcelona had said her eldest son got so anxious when told of their intentions to travel that he vomited for days. Victoria and I steeled ourselves for Sam's objections. We suspected he wouldn't react well to the massive change we were about to lay on him. He was a bright student who thrived on routine and structure, and we knew the sabbatical that we were about to hit him with would rock his world.

Sam sat across from us at a small, Formica-topped table. The pancakes he ordered had just arrived, and he casually sipped his Coke.

"Daddy and I need to talk to you about something," Victoria said. "It's kind of big news, and we're really excited about it."

I didn't wait for Sam to respond. "I'm going to leave work for a while. We're going to take a long break and live in a foreign country."

Victoria had prepared a list of sales points. Sam was a serious student and driven to get into a top college. She was concerned that Sam would resist anything that distracted him from his goal. Now without Sam uttering a word, she launched right into her pitch.

"I promise you that while we're away, school will be easier than Ramaz. It will be a great break from all the pressure. At a minimum, if you do well academically, your grades will count for college. Worst case, if you do poorly, the grades can be explained away and ignored by college admissions offices. I've already spoken to your college guidance counselor. She assured me that a semester abroad would have zero negative impact on your college applications in a few years. In fact, it may help you. Plus, apart from math and Spanish, there's little in ninth grade that you'll need to do well in tenth."

Sam had stopped chewing his food. He stared blankly at Victoria.

"We haven't told your siblings yet. We wanted you to be the first to know."

Devastating silence.

Finally: "Wait. What?"

"We're not moving for good, just spring semester and the summer."

"Where did you say we were going?"

"Mendoza, Argentina."

The background noise of tinkling cutlery suddenly came into sharp relief. Victoria and I waited for more from Sam, but he said nothing. He finished his lunch in a somber state and then asked to be excused so that he could walk around on his own.

I turned to Victoria. "What just happened?"

∿

A few days later, Sam asked to speak privately to Victoria and me. "Can I come back for camp in the summer?"

Victoria shot the final arrow in her quiver. "Absolutely." She had no idea how that would be arranged. She would sort out the details later. Besides, she hoped, Sam might change his mind once we were abroad. Sam had warmed to the idea. He came to appreciate that the trip might actually be fun, especially if colleges wouldn't look askance at it. He began to think of sabbatical as a long vacation and drummed up his own enthusiasm for it.

Victoria turned to me. "Let's hold off on telling the other kids. They don't need to know yet."

ᔎ

Mendoza was the center of Argentina's winemaking district and rested at the foothills of the Andes. We imagined it as the Napa Valley of Latin America, with great food; delicious, inexpensive wine; and long roads on which we could cycle for hours. The notion of disappearing into this world for the better part of a year was exhilarating. It ticked all the boxes: South of the equator, Mendoza basked in summer's lazy days while New York shivered in winter's doldrums; our kids would dramatically improve their Spanish skills; the Andes were a stone's throw away; there were lots of places to visit in South America. And who could resist living in a wine region?

Victoria tracked down a relocation consultant, and in July, we farmed our kids out to friends for a weekend and boarded a LAN Airlines plane bound for Mendoza via Santiago to check it out in advance of moving our family.

It didn't take long to discover that Mendoza wasn't Napa Valley. Napa was a pastoral place, geographically confined to a relatively small region. The winemaking district of Argentina had no such constraints. It was huge, and many of the vineyards were the size of large industrial farms. The roads were shoulderless, with poor asphalt conditions for road cycling. Local cyclists told us that even areas suitable for road bikes were unsafe because of crime. When we chatted with locals about their country, they spat vitriol about the corrupt political leadership.

Argentina seemed to be sliding backward. If we were looking for a dynamic part of the world for our kids to experience, Argentina certainly wasn't it. To cap our disappointment, the flight schedule to and from the airport was light. There were a few nonstop flights to Buenos Aires and Santiago, but nearly every other destination in South America would require complex travel logistics.

During our last night in Mendoza, over an inexpensive bottle of a local wine, I turned to Victoria. "I've had a lovely time. The food and wine are fantastic, and the mountains are beautiful. But there's no way we can live here."

She gazed off into the night for a few moments. "It's not perfect, but I know we can still make it work."

"Not a chance."

The next day, we hightailed it home to New York with more questions than answers.

♏︎

It was August, and Victoria drummed her fingers on our kitchen table. She was a planner and a doer. Not only would she plan vacations a full year ahead of time, but for as long as I'd known her, she also always had a running task list in her mind. While I could ruminate over trivial household purchases, she plowed ahead, got things done, and moved on to the next. She had resigned as president of the community center board and announced she would leave by the end of June. Meanwhile, she was working hard to prepare a friend and community member to take her place. Now she was getting impatient, not just with the slow progress of our sabbatical plans, but with me.

"We leave New York in December," she said tersely. "Where are we going?"

I felt the pit of my belly tighten. It was getting late, and I had no backup plan. I wondered if I was inadvertently sabotaging the situation because I was nervous about taking a break and throwing it all away. As I had done so many times before, through sheer will, I recommitted. If I was going to take a risk, I needed to be wholehearted about it.

My brother, Norm, suggested that I consider Bali, Indonesia, and reach out to his friend Richard who had lived in there in the

1980s, when both he and my brother had been part of a cohort sent to Asia on a fellowship sponsored by the Luce Foundation.

When I called Richard, his enthusiasm for Bali leapt out. "I'm telling you, Ben, it's heaven on earth." I could practically see the tears well up in his eyes as he talked to me about Bali. I asked him more about what it was like to live there.

With about 250 million people, Indonesia was the most populated Muslim country in the world. The country's tiny island of Bali, consisting of about four million people, was mostly Hindu. "The Balinese are just about the friendliest people on earth," he said. "They could be telling you that their mother died and say it with a smile." He went on to describe the island, its powerful culture, and the expatriate experience there.

I was skeptical. Elizabeth Gilbert's *Eat, Pray, Love* had recently been published and connected broadly with readers around the world. With Bali being the final destination of her journey, I was concerned that the Island of the Gods, as Bali was known, had become a cliché or, worse, a circus. As my objections mounted, I considered the possibility that something in me was resisting going on sabbatical altogether. I asked Richard whether Bali had become overrun in the aftermath of Gilbert's book.

"Absolutely not. Honestly, Ben, you can't go wrong."

"What'll I do all day?"

"Anything you want. Scuba dive, surf. You can write, read, or just hang out. Lots of foreigners live there, all doing their own thing. You won't be lonely."

I asked about a school for our kids.

"Check out Green School. A Canadian entrepreneur just built it. I don't remember his name, but it can't be hard to find on the web."

After hanging up, I researched the school on the internet. It took some digging to find Green School, but Google came through. The school's mission statement talked about joy, leadership, and teaching kids to be global citizens. There were links to news segments about the school on BBC, CNN, and ABC, along with a TED talk the founder had presented.

I showed the website to Victoria. She got the feeling we might be onto something. That night, she called the school expecting the regular runaround we had grown used to in New York: a rigorous application process for each of our four children that we would need to begin immediately if we had any hope of having our kids attending in a few months. What were the odds that they could accommodate all our children?

Ben McCrory, the head of admissions, casually said, "Sure. We've got space for your kids. How can I help?" Ben hailed from Greenwich Village. He was one of our own, and we were in.

"This time," Victoria said to me, "no recon trip. We're going to make a decision and live with it. We'll make it great." Within a few days, we had contracts signed with the school, sent in our deposit, and contacted a real estate agent that McCrory had recommended to find a place to live.

We told Sam about our change of plans. By now, he'd come to see the sabbatical as a chance to slow down and not obsess about grades. Still, if he was excited, he didn't show it. He shrugged. "Cool."

It was time to let the other children in on the plan. Victoria had earlier planted a seed in Rita's mind to ask me to take some time off from work. She tried to make it seem to Rita as if it were her own idea. Rita was having a tough time in school, and I played along every time she suggested we move to Mexico for six months. If only we could find a baseball team for Oliver to join while away, she offered, we would be set.

One by one, we told them. We showed them photos of Green School to get them excited, but the whole scheme fell flat. We pitched it as a family adventure. Nava wasn't buying it. She didn't want to leave her friends and teachers. Oliver was so horrified that he cried himself to sleep. And Rita, despite Victoria's plans, had trouble processing the information. She remained speechless for days. Victoria and I hoped the kids would eventually come around, but they weren't making things easy.

Back at the office, too, the mood was less than joyful. The board of Take-Two had turned down my request to return to the top leadership role of that company. I couldn't blame them. The CEO taking a leave of absence for an extended period must have hit them as goofy in the extreme, and this company had too much volatile history to tolerate more of it. While I hoped I could return to Take-Two, I realized it was a long shot and accepted that I would have to leave permanently. Still, I found it difficult because I had grown fond of the company and the people who worked so hard to make it great.

The company's announcement of my departure was straight-forward. There was no trying to spin this news. Their CEO was stepping down to take time to travel in Asia with his family. It was so bizarre, as the truth often is, that the raw facts made the story immediately credible.

From the team at Take-Two, some of the reactions were more positive than I'd expected. Some told me they admired my deci-sion and that it was refreshing to see a CEO who could step away from bigger, better, faster.

One day, I walked into the stainless-steel elevator of our headquarters on Broadway. Just before the door closed, the head of one of our business units jumped in. He gave me an uncer-tain smile and seemed to have something on his mind. After the elevator ascended several floors, he turned to me. "I just want to say I think what you're doing is really cool. You're making a statement, putting family ahead of work."

My announcement invited others outside the company to open up in similar ways. At lunch one day, I ran into a colleague from another firm with whom we had engineered several deals. He was known, as well as for his astute business acuity, as an acid-tongued cynic who spared neither foe nor friend. He gave me a crooked smile. "I hear you're getting out." That wasn't how

I saw it, but I let it go and braced myself for whatever came next. He patted my shoulder. "Better too early than too late."

Over and over, I had discussions with professionals in various industries who normally wore the masks required of them in their jobs but now suddenly revealed themselves and proclaimed that what they did for a living was not who they were in their souls. What surprised me most was not what these people said but the number of them who said it. So many of them did not have their whole hearts in their work, the very place they spent the bulk of their waking hours and adult years. They were not leading their lives as fully as they wanted.

Then I checked one of our stock's message board—always a mistake for any CEO who cares about affirmation, for there's never any love on those boards. Not everyone was supportive. I suspected some were simply perplexed by my behavior. By walking away from a dream job and all its financial rewards, I was pulling at the hem of incentive systems that clothed many business relationships. It was difficult for some to understand.

Some of the conversations I had were fraught and contentious. But I was already beginning to experiment with a new way of thinking and conducting myself. Grabbing as much as I could seemed at odds with a set of values I was only beginning to articulate to myself, the virtue in understanding the needs and wants of the people around me, even those with whom I competed. It was a value that rejected a zero-sum way of living—what goes into my pocket must necessarily come out of somebody else's—in search of something more expansive. I was beginning to recognize that constantly striving to get ahead over the years slowly gnawed at a more humanistic set of values. Outwardly, I maintained a firm position, but I felt the edge had already begun to come off.

ॐ

One evening, walking down Broadway on my way home, I caught a few words of passersby talking on their phones as they hurried past. "I know, I'm late, I'm sorry." "Sounds good, but I've got an evening meeting." "Don't drop the price yet; you'll look desperate." I'd never paid much attention to the conversations of strangers, mostly because I was almost always engaged in my own pointed discussion with some invisible person on the other end of a wireless connection. Suddenly, I became attuned not only to the world around me but also to my own behavior. The conversations I overheard often related to scheduling—social events, family, and meetings—or money, often in the context of real estate or other deals. Those phone conversations were just as my own had been, but my mindset had shifted. I took note and wondered how I must have sounded to others listening willy-nilly to my passing words. I wondered how many of my waking hours, including those spent wide eyed in the nighttime darkness of our bedroom, were spent focusing on matters that once were desperately urgent but now, suddenly, seemed mundane.

〰

Our travel plans firmed up. We slipped in a detour to Africa for a two-week safari. Africa was a place we'd fantasized about visiting, but we could never find the time. Now with Africa more or less on the route to Bali, we saw the opportunity and, with it, a way to get Nava, who loved animals, revved up about the trip.

We had eight months of sabbatical ahead of us, which to me seemed like an enormous amount of time but to Victoria far too short. She knew that when we returned home, the pace of our lives would again become as relentless as it was now. She fretted that the time away would pass too quickly, and she desperately wanted us to slow down.

I wondered aloud, as I often did, "But what am I going to do with my time?"

Victoria had a quick retort: "You're going to slow down. Maybe you'll do nothing. If it means being bored, so be it. Boredom is a luxury." The idea of doing nothing was difficult for me to bear.

"What about you?" I said. "What will you do?"

She seemed surprised I'd asked. Was I really that patriarchal? "Don't worry," she said. "I'll have plenty to do."

♒

One day, Oliver returned home from school. "My teacher yelled at me today. I felt bad. But then I thought, hey, only two more months and I'm outta here."

When Sam blithely mentioned to his best friend in school as they passed each other in the hallway that we would be moving to Indonesia, his friend said, "Okay," then turned to call behind him, "Whoa! What?"

In time, Rita saw our trip to Bali as an escape from a class of girls that bullied and pained her. "Do all girls everywhere act that way?" Her emotions were a mix of fear, excitement, and uncertain anticipation. They were also a bit raw.

"We'll find out," Victoria said. Rita went along with our plans without complaint.

♒

As the clock wound down to the end of the year, I was feeling impatient about our detour to Africa. Trained and practiced in the management of setting goals and achieving them as efficiently as possible, I thought of our trip to Tanzania and Kenya as a distraction from our plan to escape to Bali. If we were going to take our sabbatical in Southeast Asia, I wanted to get there as quickly as possible. Two weeks of looking at animals in what I thought would be a large zoo, an inauthentic commercial attraction, was a tangent. Already uncertain about how I would engage myself in Bali, I could not imagine keeping myself occupied while bumping along in a jeep on the plains of the Serengeti. But other than for a bit of grousing to Victoria, I kept my mouth shut.

We tied up loose ends and made last-minute preparations. Victoria dove into the details of visas, health forms for school, and packing up the family. She arranged to have most of our remaining belongings sent to storage to make room for the tenants who would be renting our apartment. She also told me, with a laugh and a searching look, that one of our neighbors had asked her in a whisper that day, "Is it too late for Ben to change his mind?"

We inoculated ourselves against hepatitis and yellow fever. A few days before we left, Victoria, the kids, and I gathered in the kitchen and made a ceremony of taking our first doses of Malarone to protect us from malaria. We each raised a glass of water, popped the pill, and drank to our adventure ahead.

ᔕᘉ

The night before we left, I had dinner with one of my partners, Jordan. As I made my way to the nearby restaurant, light snowflakes shimmied to the ground, a precursor of a fierce blizzard that was making its way up the East Coast and threatened to block our escape from winter.

There had been so much tension for me in my partnership that I welcomed the chance for casual conversation. We met in a small Greenwich Village restaurant. Jordan had an openness in conversation that others might find uncomfortable. Before we'd even ordered, he said, "You coming back?"

"As I told the partners, I have every intention of returning."

He laughed. "A carefully worded answer. Do you think you really will?"

The perspectives of time and distance often lead to insight that causes people to change course. I secretly hoped the sabbatical might light the way to a radical change in my life and my family's and alter our lives permanently. Perhaps it would bring us to a different way of being. I did not know the answer. All I knew was that I needed some distance.

I smiled and shrugged. "In these situations, one never knows." I expected another laugh but got a thoughtful nod.

At the end of the dinner, Jordan presented me with a small going-away gift, a Leatherman pocket multitool. "I figure you may need this on the road. You'll be ready for anything."

I shot him a puzzled look. I got the feeling he didn't know quite what to make of what I was doing. Still, in the context of his desire to grow the firm, I thought he wanted to ensure that the firm's cofounder would return. In business, small gifts were common, often as a tool to establish a closer connection. I was touched by his gift and accepted it with gratitude. It reminded me that for all the economic reasons people enter into business, commerce is also a very human affair. It requires not only reason and analysis but also emotional intelligence, social skills, and deep personal engagement. Even if we didn't see eye to eye about what I was about to do, it felt good to reaffirm our respect for each other.

Snow was sticking to the ground in New York when we zipped up the last of our bags. I pulled my coat from the closet. Victoria took it from me—to hold it for me to put on, I thought—but instead she hung it back in the closet.

"Absolutely not." Our packing list consisted only of light clothing.

Out in the hallway, Victoria turned the key to lock our apartment. We called our children to each take a bag. They hesitated and argued about who would carry what, but ultimately, with some parental prodding, each grabbed a bag and hauled it down the elevator to the lobby. We got into a car that took us to JFK.

We worked our way through traffic and then the airport to get to our gate while the snowfall grew heavier. As we waited for our flight to be called, we heard the words we feared. An agent announced our flight would be delayed. My heart sank, but half a second later, I recovered. There was no rush. For the first time in a long while, there was no place I needed to be. Although

I had no interest in spending more time than necessary at the airport, I let the delay wash over me. I didn't get tense or race to find an alternative flight scheduled to leave earlier. I just let it go.

One hour later, through fierce snowfall, our plane's wheels lifted off the runway, leaving behind a historic blizzard, one that would eventually drop twenty inches of snow and embroil the mayor's office in a controversy about the speed of snow removal. When I read about it from afar, I was glad to have it in the rear-view mirror.

four | 3

We flew from New York to Tanzania via Ethiopia. During our layover at Addis Ababa Bole International Airport, Victoria found a quiet row of airport seats, settled in, and cracked open an enormous volume, Vikram Seth's *A Suitable Boy*. The kids too pulled out some reading material. We had bought them Kindle readers precisely for situations like this. They were lightweight for travel but filled with material to keep the kids occupied.

I was fidgety. I felt the impulse to reach into my pocket for my phone to check for emails, like an amputee's urge to scratch a phantom limb. There were no messages. No deals, meetings, or conference calls. Colleagues from work no longer needed to be in touch with me. Suddenly untethered from the comfort and tyranny of constant contact, I didn't quite know what to do with myself. I was free from my email in-box that seemed to refill as quickly as I decanted it, but I felt slightly lonely too. Instead of chatter, there was dead silence.

I wandered around the airport, looking for something to buy, something to do. I searched for a coffee shop, hoping for a Starbucks. Instead, I found a dingy one filled with stale cigarette smoke. I continued on and came upon an ATM. When I inserted my card, an error message on the screen said that the machine was out of cash. I wandered some more, looking for a newsstand, but came up empty.

When our flight was called after three long hours of fidgeting, it was a mad dash to the gate. Passengers swarmed and overwhelmed the gate attendant. Compared to this general chaos, JFK was a well-oiled machine. Tired and agitated, we eventually found our way to our seats.

From Addis Ababa we traveled to Arusha, Tanzania, a gateway city to the Serengeti National Park. Our guide, Abu, with whom we had prearranged a pickup, met us at the airport. Dressed in khaki shorts, khaki boots, and a button-down khaki shirt, the slight Tanzanian man welcomed us warmly and led us toward the parking lot. On the way, I stopped at a telecom kiosk and bought a local prepaid SIM card for my phone. Victoria picked up some vegetarian *ugali*, a thick porridge of maize-meal flour and spinach-like greens. Although the other kids turned up their noses, Sam scarfed it down. His picky eating habits had their limits in the face of hunger.

Abu showed us to his Land Rover, another vision in khaki, and we loaded our gear onto the roof. As we drove into town, Sam pointed to Mount Kilimanjaro off to the left. It shimmered in the far distance as it climbed slowly from the plains to a plateau, where snow covered its dormant volcanic cones. Its color metamorphosed from lavender to marine blue as it rose. I stared at it and thought about a friend who had recently climbed the mountain, and I imagined for a moment the challenge of climbing a mountain myself.

Abu pointed to small sand tornadoes in the middle distance, swirling whirlwinds that sucked dust into their updrafts. Sam stared at the odd sight, lost in his own thoughts.

When we arrived at our lodging and dumped our bags, I checked again for emails, but there was no wireless connection. The SIM card was useless. About to head into the wilderness with just my family and Abu, I was utterly cut off from my world back home.

〰

Before we headed into the national park, Victoria asked if we could visit a local school. We had wanted our trip to be educational for our kids, for them to understand environments vastly different from their own and how other kids lived in them.

Abu took us to nearby Shepherds Junior School and introduced us to the principal, who gladly showed us around and brought us into a classroom to introduce us to the kids. Victoria stood at the head of the class.

"Good morning, grade seven," she said to a class of twenty-five kids, all in neat school uniforms.

"Good morning!" they all answered in unison.

Victoria led a discussion with the kids and directed their questions to our children. "What are your hobbies?" one child asked.

"I play baseball," Oliver said. Victoria demonstrated with an imaginary bat. When we moved on to a third-grade class, Victoria led a round of "If You're Happy and You Know It." It was cute, and I was impressed to see how seriously the local kids seemed to take our visit.

On the way back to our hotel, Nava tugged at Victoria and whined in a faux baby voice, "When are we going to see the animals, Mommy?"

"Tomorrow, Nava. I promise. And you don't need to talk in that voice."

The next day, Abu drove us to the national park. He rolled back the Land Rover's canvas roof, and the park's measureless azure sky opened to us. Grassy plains stretched as far as the horizon. As we bumped along the Serengeti, its vastness made me lightheaded. The plains, solitary and isolated, reminded me that I was as far from New York as I could have imagined.

As we came upon a tower of giraffes, Abu stopped the car and killed the engine. In the profound absence of human noise, I listened to the sound of giraffes brushing against the bush and nibbling at leaves. They walked so awkwardly yet so beautifully.

I stared at them and then turned my gaze to my children and Victoria. Oliver stared in awe. Nava whooped. They watched in wonder for a long while. I took as much pleasure in them as I did in the wildlife. Something was already changing in me, though I could not quite place it.

Abu asked, "May I proceed?" The Land Rover shuddered and thrummed. We were off.

Thirty minutes later Abu stopped, again cut the engine, and pointed toward two o'clock. "Do you see?" I didn't. I was playing with the settings of our digital camera. "Keep looking," he said as I lifted my gaze. A slight rustling crackled in the distance. The entire family shifted from their seats over to the right side of the vehicle and jostled for a good view. The sound grew into a more elaborate crunching, almost a racket. A herd of elephants emerged from the bush.

The sheer size of the animals astounded me. Nava and Rita almost jumped for joy. Victoria froze. Nava quickly reached into her backpack and took out Eli, her stuffed elephant doll. She held Eli as high as her tiny three-foot frame allowed and yelled to the herd, "It's your cousin!"

Abu rolled his *R*s in a thick Tanzanian accent. "May I proceed?" He kicked the vehicle into gear, and we lurched forward.

Abu was an endearing man who possessed an encyclopedic knowledge of the natural history of the area. He spooled it out carefully so as not to overwhelm us, speaking deliberately and precisely. Every spoken word conveyed exactly the meaning he intended. He was simultaneously authoritative and polite. He was solicitous of us, especially of the children, but mostly he was interested in educating us about the wonders of the East African bush, the extraordinary mammal migrations, and their endless search for water and nutrition.

As one day on safari bled into the next, the Serengeti and Ngorongoro parks worked their magic on all of us. Or almost all.

A few days into our trip, Oliver became depressed. More than his siblings, he had an unusually close group of school friends, about four or five boys, whom he missed terribly. It was beginning to dawn on him that he wouldn't see them for a long time. That he had his family to keep him company did not console him. With his birthday approaching and his head hung low, his demeanor was a stark contrast to that of his siblings, who were boisterous with excitement about the animals. The night of his birthday, I led him out of his tent toward the dining tent. The darkness outside was as black as Oliver's mood. I heard a snort from an animal we could not see but sounded so close I could practically feel its breath.

I said to Oliver in a low voice, "Quickly. Let's move." We hurried our pace and arrived at the lighted dining tent, about a hundred yards away. Our Maasai hosts greeted us, dressed in traditional red *shuka* fabric, cell phones attached to their hips.

At dinner, Oliver was still feeling down. "How about a game of ghost?" Victoria said. It was a word game in which each player adds a letter to a word being formed. The string must be a fragment of a real word but not yet a whole word; the player who first forms a complete word loses the round. Oliver said, "Only if I don't sit next to Sam." Sam liked to prey on Oliver, thinking of letters that would force Oliver to lose.

Sam opened the game.

"*M.*"

"*M* or *N*?" Victoria asked.

"*M*, like Mets."

"That's not helpful, Sam."

A group of servers ultimately came to Oliver's rescue. Singing "Happy Birthday" in Swahili, they presented him with a small birthday cake, candles ablaze. As a reminder of the resiliency of children, a smile returned to Oliver's face.

Wake-up on safari was generally at six o'clock, and Sam was always the first to jump out of bed. I wondered where the teenage son who loved his sleep had gone. I thought Sam was deeply incurious about anything he couldn't view on a screen, text on a phone, or manipulate with a video game controller.

If something did attract his interest, it was never before noon. Any attempt at conversation earlier than that was a struggle met with mutterings and mumbles. In the morning he did not so much walk as stumble, loose shoelaces whipping around like spaghetti.

Now Sam awoke with a start. He was playing with our small digital camera and conjuring up ways to create a fun video about our trip, creating shot lists and choreographing them with his siblings and us. When, on our final day of safari, Abu offered one last dawn roam on the plains, Sam was the first to volunteer. I was beginning to see enthusiasm from a kid who, in New York, couldn't manage to utter a verb at the dinner table. Now I even caught a glimpse of emerging creativity.

Nava was wide eyed and hungry for knowledge about the animals. When Abu spoke, she whipped out a notebook and pencil from her knapsack. When she had filled a few pages on hippopotami, gannets, baboons, zebras, hyenas, and wildebeests, Sam encouraged her to create a video so that she could share her experience with her first-grade friends at home. At a time when polished online videos were only beginning to become popular, Sam directed Nava anchoring a newsreel video on our small digital camera and later helped her edit it on our MacBook. The gap left from the two front teeth that had fallen out was clearly visible when she began earnestly, "This is Nava Feder reporting from the Serengeti on African animals."

Although Rita was excited about the animals and being on a family adventure, at night her thoughts turned to entering a new school and whether the kids there, like some of those back home, would bully her. In the last few days on safari, with the prospect of the first day of school approaching, Rita was getting visibly agitated. Victoria asked her to focus on the family and the adventure we were undertaking. One night, Rita wrote a song with a sweet but doleful melody that she called "It Hurts on the Inside."

I have a great family,
And I know that's always true,
But sometimes my heart goes the other way.

I'm proud of myself and so are others.
But when I get teased,
I consider it true.

It hurts on the inside,
It hurts on the outside.
When I think of myself, I get so confused.

I was glad she could express her feelings but saddened that she was in that state. I put my arm around her small shoulders and curled her in for a hug. I didn't always have the words to console her, but I tried to make her feel safe and loved. She wriggled from my embrace.

For me, the Serengeti's majestic beauty and teeming wildlife astounded the imagination. It practically begged me to ponder a world long gone. It took me three or four days in the bush to realize I hadn't seen a single jet contrail in the vast Serengeti sky. The last time I had experienced that was on 9/11, when aviation authorities banned all flights for days. On the African plains, my sense of what was real in the world expanded and opened me to a renewed sense of wonder, which I had slowly lost over many years.

It was the terrain's vastness, its oceans of grass, that really soothed me. It not only sustained the millions of migrating mammals but also focused my attention and calmed my mind. I stared for long periods into the far distance, where the greensward met a cerulean sky in a curved horizon.

Abu tried to explain the intricate details. The grass grew from mostly shallow soil that occasionally dropped to levels deep enough to allow a lonely acacia tree to sink its roots and spread its canopy. The wide variety of herbivores that lived in various states of symbiosis—some ate the top of the grass, others the bottom; one evolved mandibles that chomped, another that grinded; one listened for predators, the other sniffed for them—conveyed to me a world in balance. Even when one mammal killing another seemed to violate it, that was part of the balance too. It was an endlessly complex ecological system in which both plants and the animals that fed on them coevolved.

The other tourists on the savannah detracted from my experience. They were attracted to the big game and, morbidly, fresh kills. When word spread on the rangers' radios that there was blood on the soil, they came racing from all corners of the park. While most everyone else on safari was looking for big game and dramatic action, I secretly wished we would come up empty. I sought serenity. I took pleasure in poking my head out of the open roof of our Land Rover, even as it barreled across the plains, and standing there entranced, taking in the scene as the wind and landscape rushed by. The Serengeti made New York and our lives there seem remote. I felt tensions ease, anxiety fall away, and in their place, a connection to something grounded in the primordial life of the Serengeti, the eternal cycles of animal migrations, and reminders of the steady march of evolution.

So much of my life in New York was spent living in a world of abstraction: navigating legal and regulatory rules of the game, constructing and operating within complex commercial arrangements, and generally moving pieces on the corporate strategic chessboard. I focused only on the most essential elements and discarded the details of anything that did not fit into the myopia I had deliberately cultivated.

Despite attempts to look at the big picture, focus was the only way to declutter my mind and get things done. Mostly I had walked with my head cocked downward, reading and responding to emails, my thumbs tapping at the diminutive keyboard in the way hens peck at seed. I didn't notice anything. Here, on the Serengeti, I raised my head to look straight ahead and lifted my

gaze to a horizon that, for me, had long since disappeared in the
canyons of Manhattan's long avenues.

I remembered a well-publicized Harvard study in which
researchers asked subjects to watch a short video of two groups of
people passing a basketball around. The subjects were told either
to count the number of passes made by one of the teams or to
keep count of bounce passes versus aerial passes. After watching
the video and reporting their counts, the subjects were asked
if they saw anything out of the ordinary take place. Most said no.
They then watched the video again, this time with instructions
not to count anything but just to relax and watch. In the midst
of the video, an actor wearing a full gorilla suit saunters across
the set, taking time to turn to the camera and pound his chest.
The surprised subjects said they were so busy tallying passes
that they did not see the gorilla. I imagined that in New York, I
would have been in that group. Now I was widening my awareness, hoping to see the gorillas.

∿

On our last day on safari, we waited next to the Land Rover at
an airstrip and, like survivors marooned on an island, scanned
the skies for an airplane. We were headed out of the bush for the
Tanzanian coastal island of Zanzibar, our final stop before Bali.
By then, I was ready to leave the Serengeti. The need for new
stimulation and moving on to the next thing, which both fed me
and drove me mad in New York, pulled at me again.

At the airstrip, we were the only passengers in sight. A small
dot appeared on the horizon and grew as it approached, accom-
panied by a rising rumble of propellers. A small, old, twin-engine
bush plane landed and taxied to the Land Rover. The pilot, a
thirtysomething Canadian man sporting aviator sunglasses and
the familiar khaki outfit, dropped a ladder from the cockpit
and popped out. He loaded our bags in the hold while we said
our warm good-byes to Abu. We piled into the passenger cabin
through the rear door.

The plane shuddered as it accelerated down the runway. The noise was deafening. Victoria mock-gritted her teeth and looked at me as if to ask, "Is this hunk of metal going to make it?" I shrugged. The kids howled with joy at the adventure. We rose, banked left, and winged toward a misty mountain ridge, clearing it with what seemed to me only inches to spare. Victoria pulled a nervous smile. This was unlike any plane or flight we had ever taken, and the young pilot, who was in Tanzania logging miles on his way to a commercial pilot's license, did not inspire confidence.

I eventually settled into the flight and reflected on our time in the Serengeti. At a time in my life when I was searching for meaning, the predation of the wild, the endless pursuit of food and shelter, the birthing and protecting of young in order to propagate genes, seemed at once both elemental and pointless.

As beautiful as the Serengeti was, if I was lacking a sense of meaning in my life, I did not find it there, at the very base of the pyramid of human priorities. But the Serengeti did remind me of the necessity of attending to basic needs without which meaning, beyond simple genetic propagation, was impossible.

〰️

When we landed in Zanzibar, the poverty of the place crashed into our world. Small huts, constructed of mud and elephant dung, lined the roads. Other structures were made of shoddy-looking, fissure-riddled brick. Everywhere, we saw partially built homes with walls but no roofs, frames but no windows, foundations but no floors. Often the bush reclaimed the foundation altogether so that instead of a living room taking shape, an acacia tree sprouted. Meager cattle and goats small enough to be mistaken for dogs roamed freely in the streets. Families grew vegetables near their huts in small patches of subsistence farms. Women by the side of the road sold just about anything: a few pieces of fruit, bundles of firewood, bald tires, you name it.

I had the resources to be able to take time off—although not to drop out of my career altogether. While I was not living from hand to mouth in the way a lot of people do, I did take significant career risks by doing what I did. But they paled in insignificance beside the poverty of Zanzibar. Yet I couldn't say that most of the people here looked unhappier than Manhattanites.

The prize of Zanzibar was the port city of Stone Town, which attracted young backpackers with its tight, meandering alleyways peppered with art galleries and mosques. Tourists filled the restaurants and flopped on the pillows of hookah lounges.

At five thirty in the morning, I woke to the sound of the muezzin. I appreciated the music of the place and the sweet, soaring song of the Muslim call to prayer. Perhaps my own traditional Jewish background helped me appreciate the song of supplication. It was a glimpse into the softer, easy spirit of the place that I had imagined.

In Africa, my family and I began sharing our day-to-day experiences, both the searing and the mundane. For my children, it was an opportunity to observe and ask questions about a world that was utterly foreign to their Manhattan experience. For all of us, simply eating dinner together every night, a practice that had been lost to us in New York, seemed to matter a lot. In the evenings, we played Boggle and other games to fight boredom and distract the kids from periodic bickering. Inspired by the Serengeti, Sam ramped up his predatory gamesmanship.

∿

From Zanzibar we flew to Doha, Qatar, for an overnight layover on our way to Bali. If the airport in Ethiopia was a jolting introduction to the developing world, the transfer lounge in Doha inflicted a shock of material excess. It was reminiscent of some of the best hotels I'd stayed in as part of the trappings of traveling for a large company. Out of the corner of his eye, Oliver saw a lounge for kids that featured free video game consoles. He shouted in excitement, dropped his bag, and ran. The other kids gave chase. Victoria and I took turns for the first hot shower we'd had in a long time. We sat down for a meal in the lounge while we waited for our next flight.

On the plane, Victoria and I talked about Rita. We were worried about her. We hoped the situation in her new school would be different and she wouldn't feel bullied. By the time we'd boarded, I'd already noticed a change in the way our kids related to each other and how we behaved as a family. Sam was engaging more. Nava began to lose her baby-like way of speaking. Oliver and Rita were getting along better than they had been in New York. It seemed to have dawned on our children that for the next long while, they might have only each other as company.

five ③

T he percussive thrum of gamelan, Bali's traditional music, piped through the airport speakers greeted us as we stumbled off the plane in Denpasar, Bali. Exhausted by two days of travel, we ambled through the airport's corridors to the immigration hall. A large sign notified us that we needed to pay a tax to enter the country, payable at a cashier's desk only in Indonesian rupiah, the sole access to which was an ATM beyond the customs borderline. Victoria had planned ahead and had already exchanged currency. We headed to the long queue of travelers waiting to be processed by customs and immigration.

As we drew closer to the customs counter, I saw a German man hand over a fifty-dollar bill to a customs official who slid it into his pocket and stamped the man's passport with quick efficiency. In all my business travel, I had never seen such a blatant bribe, but I knew enough to keep quiet. I resisted the temptation to elbow Victoria and say, "Did you see that?" A split-second calculation of stakes, upside and downside, made me wonder if I might one day need that trick.

When we exited baggage claim, Oliver spotted, amid the throng, our handwritten name on a placard. We approached the man holding the sign, who flashed a wide, toothy grin and introduced himself as Nyoman. He was the manager of the home we rented. He led us to his car, and we piled in. He'd brought along a friend with a second car to deal with our bags.

We drove out of the airport toward Ubud, a town at the base of the dormant volcano Mount Batur. As we made our way, we peered out the windows at a dirty urban sprawl: strewn garbage, traffic, and discount retail outlets. Large billboards shouted brands like Rip Curl and Billabong. Smoke filled the air and burned our throats. Bali seemed denuded of the verdant rice paddies and carved irrigation canals I'd seen on the internet. In their place, rivers of motorbikes streamed along, some with whole families of four or five riding the saddle. The irrigation canals that channeled water from the highlands were consolidated into large rivers, dug deep, banked by concrete, and filled with refuse. The feeling creeping up on me was reminiscent of a postapocalyptic video game I had considered developing.

Driving on cracked, unlit roads, it took an hour to reach Ubud. One house we passed as we drove into town had about two dozen motorcycles parked outside. "Someone having a party?" I asked Nyoman.

"Oh, no, Mr. Ben," he said politely. "Someone died, and the villagers are there to be with the family and show respect."

I made a mental note to pause before I made any more cultural assumptions. But the sheer number of motorcycles said something about the communal support this family must have received. I couldn't help contrasting it with the more insular way I lived. I flashed to my father's funeral two decades earlier and the outpouring of love I witnessed there, then for a split second imagined my own funeral and wondered about the size of the crowd, as if somehow it would measure the success of my life.

Just beyond Ubud lay the village of Junjugan, where Victoria had rented what the local real estate agent marketed as *Villa Tirta Tawar*, Holy Spring Villa. We pulled up to a house surrounded by a high security wall.

Nyoman tooted the horn, a night watchman opened the iron gate, and we drove through the gateway to the front door. Nyoman killed the engine. Victoria called out, "Everyone please take a bag." Our children had become seasoned travelers, and none of them complained. Even Nava pulled her weight, taking whatever bag her little body could lift.

Nyoman entered first, spotted a large spider on the terracotta floor, and instead of squashing it, quickly shooed it out the door. "Please, before you come in, take off your shoes."

Dim light fell on the floor of the shadowy entranceway. "Can we turn on some lights, Nyoman?" I asked.

"They are on, Mr. Ben." Electricity was expensive in Bali, and extra wattage came at a premium.

Nyoman showed us around. One wing of the boomerang-shaped villa had two bedrooms with queen-sized beds, each adorned by mosquito netting. The other wing had a Japanese-style dining area with an elevated platform, a low-slung table, and cushions on which to sit. The walls facing the interior of the boomerang were made of glass and opened to the back garden and patio, not visible in the night.

We walked outside to a separate small building a few steps away that housed the small kitchen and laundry. A third bedroom was in yet another building, again just a few steps away. The boys would share that room.

"Please keep the doors locked to both buildings," Nyoman said.

Victoria frowned. "Must we? What if they need to come to us in the middle of the night?"

"It's for safety, Miss Victoria."

We worked out a serviceable system of keys that allowed the boys to come get us if they needed to and vice versa.

When he finished the brief tour, Nyoman smiled and said in a Balinese singsong way, "I'll go home now. I'll return in the morning, yah?" We were alone in our dark home, feeling more than a little lost.

We put our tired children to bed, careful to drape the mosquito netting around their beds the way we had learned in Africa. Malaria had been eradicated in Bali, but dengue fever, also carried by mosquitos, had not. It was an extremely painful and potentially fatal disease.

The kids were asleep in minutes. In total silence, Victoria and I collapsed on the benches in the living area. On the dining table sat a bowl filled with fruit I couldn't name, a gift from the real estate agent who had insisted we pay rent for our entire stay in advance. In the dappled light and with the experience of that grim ride from the airport still crackling in my mind, the full weight of our situation fell on me hard. I turned to Victoria.

"What the fuck did we do?"

Victoria never let me see her sweat. "Remember your twenty-four-hour rule," she said in a level-headed way that I knew hid her own nervousness. Whenever I got some phone call or email that felt like someone had just dropped a steaming problem in my lap and made me feel exposed, before I reacted or tried to find a solution, I gave the situation twenty-four hours to percolate. Better yet, I tried to find a distraction. Somehow, solutions always presented themselves as my unconscious mind worked the problem.

We turned off the lights and went to bed, cocooned in the mosquito netting. I slept fitfully.

〰️

The next morning, I woke ahead of everyone else. Bright sunlight shone through the glass patio doors. I shuffled out of our bedroom, careful not to wake Victoria. I heard the trill and warble of birdsong. I stepped outside and saw a lush green backyard that shimmered in the sunlight. A rooster crowed in the distance. The faint sound of running water gurgled from just outside the walled border of the backyard. A small swimming pool sparkled, and a hardwood gazebo invited quiet conversation. Beyond the walls of the property, in perfect view, curved terraces of emerald-green rice fields were carved into a round hill.

I glimpsed Nyoman in a pale-yellow polo shirt, batik sarong, and sandals. He was doing the rounds on the property, lighting incense and setting out little pallets of rattan and banana leaf filled with flower petals and bits of food. I thought he was checking the property and feeding the birds.

He smiled at me and waved. "I'm laying out morning offerings." When he was done, he put his hands together in prayer, smiled slightly, and bowed gently forward.

Victoria emerged from the bedroom just as Nyoman finished his last offering. I could see a wave of relief wash over her. With a soaring feeling of arrival, we both breathed in the beauty of what would be our home for six months. I let the bright tropical sun melt away the tensions I had felt the night before.

Nyoman introduced us to Putu, a young mother of one who cleaned the house, and then to Made, the gardener and handyman. Neither spoke any English, but they smiled and bowed in a friendly if somewhat reverential way. Putu set out some toast and cut fruit.

The kids didn't wake until late morning. One by one they emerged from their jet-lagged slumber. We introduced them to Putu and Made, but there was no time to linger. We were already late for a tour of their school, which we had arranged through Ben McCrory, the school's head of admissions. Victoria and I rushed them through a quick meal and herded them into the rental car Nyoman would drive.

On the ride to school, Nyoman drove aggressively, leaving only inches between our car and the one ahead. It didn't matter how fast he or other drivers were traveling. The braking distance on this island was obviously shorter than anywhere else on the planet because everyone drove the same way. The vehicular twerk seemed to excite local drivers.

I choked on truck exhaust and smoke that wafted in from all sides. I saw farmers burning rice chaff in their fields and villagers incinerating their household garbage by the curb. I covered my mouth and nose, lifting the collar of my T-shirt to the bridge of my nose. We passed through the center of Ubud, where a large open-air market housed merchants selling local food and tourist bric-a-brac out of individual stalls. We passed the tony village of Nyuh Kuning and through the aptly named Monkey Forest. We drove mostly in silence, Victoria and I taking in the scenery, the children paralyzed by the terror of attending a new school in a foreign country.

At last, Nyoman edged out of the tailgating competition. The ride to school, which was supposed to take twenty minutes, clocked in at forty. We were staring at a New York–style commute.

As we entered the campus, asphalt gave way to a dirt road so broken that it felt as if we were back in Africa, bouncing in a Land Rover through the rough outback of the Serengeti. We pulled up to the entrance of the school and the child drop-off zone. Two Indonesian men, dressed in orange sarongs and Balinese headdress, greeted us with expansive smiles, slight bows, and hands in prayer position at their chests. We signed in and waited to join a group of visitors about to start the tour.

John Hardy led the school tour. He and his wife, Cynthia, had founded the school a few years earlier. John, in his sixties, was a formidable creative force. He stood in front of us and told us his story. He was dyslexic, he said, and recounted how, in the Ontario town where he grew up, the disorder was poorly understood, and as a result, his dyslexia went undiagnosed and untreated. Despite his obvious intelligence and talent, he was treated like the village idiot. His school experience, as he described it, was nothing short of misery.

Almost as soon as he could, John escaped to Bali. When he arrived, he became interested in the island's jewelry-making traditions and learned the techniques of the local artisans. He developed his first pieces by applying new designs to traditional Balinese methods. He began selling his jewelry to tourists on the beaches and expanded it from there to a global operation. He and Cynthia grew their business and brand dramatically, ultimately selling his products to high-end US retailers like

Nordstrom and Saks Fifth Avenue. When he sold his business to a private equity firm, he and Cynthia used the proceeds to found Green School. John was a born salesman, magnetic, and unwavering to the core in his conviction about what he was doing and its ultimate impact on the educational experience. I wasn't sure I was buying his story.

John walked us past a new kitchen structure being built in the shape of a dragon, whose final design would be determined by a student sketch competition. He contrasted Green School with his own school experience: "The people who built the school I went to were the same people who built the prison and the insane asylum, and they built all three institutions out of the same materials. We built this school to inspire students and educators, and we built it almost entirely of renewable resources."

He pointed to an array of vegetable gardens in the near distance. "All the food we serve at Green School is grown right here, and students are responsible for its production." The place was gorgeous. But whether there was any real education going on was an open question. He made precious little mention of core subjects like math, science, or humanities.

We walked by some classrooms. There were no angles in any of the structures. Everything, including the student desks, was organically shaped. While they learned, students could hear the rush of the Ayung River in the ravine just behind the school. They could feel the tropical breeze that blew in from the nearby Indian Ocean. As we passed the Heart of School's grand curved staircase leading to the second floor, we saw children's flip-flops haphazardly piled at its base. "Green School is a barefoot environment," John said. "What we're trying to do here is to teach our kids not only the core subjects, like math, science, and English, but also to be global citizens." What he said resonated with Victoria and me. Over the years, we had debated endlessly about how to provide our children with a Jewish education, which involved a certain amount of indoctrination, and simultaneously engage their creative, explorative spirits. We struggled with the best way to prepare them to be involved in the world while maintaining their traditions.

As we walked we came upon an open well with a turbine in the center. "Our gravitation water vortex," John said. The focus of Green School's curriculum that year was water and its role in the environment. Water would be the core theme too for the way science and the humanities were taught. The water vortex, a microhydropower plant designed to provide electricity to the campus, was the school's attempt to put into practice some water-centered learning. "We want to be completely self-sufficient," John said. Then he added, without being defensive, "We're still trying to get it to work."

As we ambled along a pebble path, a tall girl with straight blond hair and blushed cheeks ran over with a friend and stopped us in our tracks. Carina's neon-green tutu matched her bright demeanor. "Are you Sam?" She exploded in a giant grin. Sam was taken aback by her exuberance. "We've been waiting for you! We've been checking you out on Facebook, and now you're here."

Her classmate Pim was from Bangkok. Green School classes were a United Nations of students. Pim tied her long, dark hair in a ponytail and smiled at Sam. "There're only four other boys in our class of thirteen." Sam turned beet red.

We ended our tour at a bamboo sign, "Healing Circle." At the circle's center was a giant smoky quartz crystal planted heavily in the ground. It stopped one of the women on the tour in her tracks.

"Wow!" She turned to me, her palms open to the crystal as if to a campfire. "Do you feel that?"

"Not really."

"I can't get any closer."

I looked at her blankly.

When the tour was over, Victoria asked the kids, "So what do you think?" No answer. By the look on their faces, we could tell that they were struck dumb by the massive differences between Green School and the education they were used to.

〜

The next day, we woke the kids at seven. Putu had arranged breakfast for us, a cocktail of fruit we were beginning to recognize: rambutan, salak, and dragon fruit. Rita and Oliver begged for another day to recover from all the travel, but Victoria was adamant. The quicker they got started, the quicker they would acclimate. By eight o'clock, we were all in the car again on our way back to school. Unlike the previous day, when we'd arrived after the school day had started, morning drop-off was a busy scene at the school's entrance. In front of us, Western-looking schoolchildren popped out of SUVs and minivans driven by Balinese drivers. Their sandals clacking away, the kids streamed through the entrance like farmed fish. Sam looked blank. Nava appeared panicked. Oliver was screwing up his courage. Rita seemed almost paralyzed with dread.

"You guys will do great," Victoria said. "Just be yourselves."

"Would you like us to come in with you?" I asked. Oliver grimaced as if that would be worse than death. But the girls were open to the idea. Oliver slid back the side door of our rented Toyota Avanza minivan. He and Sam said their good-byes and joined the flow of kids. We gave them a minute. Then Victoria and I took the girls by the hand and led them to their classrooms, leaving Nyoman to park the car.

Rita and Nava were each assigned a buddy to show them around. Rita's buddy was eager to educate her about Green School toilets. Since they were self-composting, no toilet paper was allowed. "When you finish with your business, you take a scoop of sawdust from a bucket and dump it down the toilet hole." Rita made a face. Her buddy said, "Or you can hold it in till you get home. That's what I do."

Once classes were under way, Victoria and I hung back at the *warung*, an open bamboo restaurant that served snacks and coffee and offered free Wi-Fi, a welcome amenity because broadband internet access was hard to come by and expensive. We overheard a heated discussion among some parents.

Ben McCrory bounced over. "May I introduce you to someone?"

Ben brought us over to Michelle, a nurse who was married to Andy, one of the teachers at Green School. I asked Michelle why she'd moved to Bali from Oregon. I could tell by the way she responded that, like me, she didn't have a simple answer. She was there for a host of reasons, not all of which she could or would easily articulate. But one thing was clear: even expats on modest incomes were free to enjoy a life that they otherwise couldn't afford.

"Back home," she said, "I'd spend my weekends washing laundry and cleaning house. Here, I'm free to be with friends and family and pursue my passions." Chief among these passions was mountain biking through the hills and terraced rice paddies of Bali. "Hey, do you guys cycle?" Of course we cycled, mostly road bikes, though. "It's all mountain bikes here," she said, citing the poor roads but great trails.

Green School had an informal but active mountain biking club that was always looking for new recruits. We got the full lowdown, including weekly scheduled rides (men, women, and mixed), as well as directions to the bike shop with which she had arranged a discount for Green School parents. We could be there and back by the time school let out. Then she officially inducted us into the Green School Cycling Club.

᭐

We headed to Denpasar to buy our mountain bikes. On the way, I thought about the Dutch family who never wanted to leave. Just as Sam had finished reading the *Odyssey* for school the previous semester, we had landed in our very own version of Homer's land of the lotus-eaters. I searched on my phone's browser for Homer's description and thought it could apply as easily to Bali's expats. Wayfarers who landed there "left off caring about home, and did not even want to go back and say what had happened to them, but were for staying and munching lotus with the lotus-eaters without thinking further of their return."

We returned to Green School in time for pickup. Victoria asked how school went. "It's more like camp," Oliver said. "There's no homework, hardly any tests, and lots of time outside."

Sam put on some New York swagger. "It's a total slacker school." Good, he could use the break.

Rita and I talked about "friend groups" at the school, and I could tell they reminded her of the cliques back home and made her anxious. But she also told us how she exchanged one of her Silly Bandz with a girl for a seashell from Thailand and that they were now friends. That gave us hope.

〜

The following week, Nyoman invited us to his family compound in Junjugan and from there to a local performance of a Hindu dance drama called the *Kecak*, or "Monkey Chant." Typically, three and sometimes four generations lived together as one family unit within these compounds, which were often the only assets the families possessed.

The walls that surrounded Nyoman's family compound were ornate Balinese masonry. We passed through the front entrance, a split in the wall, and through a guest pavilion that opened up into the rest of the compound. The entranceway had a backing wall that created corners, which according to Balinese legend were impassible to demons. The complex included a few living quarters, a temple, and a separate kitchen. The ground was simple, level dirt. We smelled the stench of the pig being raised in the back. They lived humbly compared to the home we rented, and I saw Nava's face fall at the sight of it. It was unexpected because of the way Nyoman showed up for work, with pressed shirt and pants and neatly combed hair.

Nyoman's wife placed her hands in a prayer position to wel-come us. Outside the main building, she motioned to us to be seated on the floor, cross-legged, the way we had observed the locals eat their meals. Nyoman's parents joined us, his father's face so weathered, it looked like fissures in jagged rock, his mother's bright with an expansive grin.

With Nyoman translating, we chitchatted. They welcomed us, total strangers, with warmth and sincerity. I commented that they all seemed to wear perpetual smiles. Nyoman explained that because canine teeth projected aggression, Balinese tradition-ally filed them down as part of a ceremony initiating children into adulthood. To me, it made their countenances irresistible and inviting.

From Nyoman's family compound, it was a short walk to the village center where the *Kecak* was being performed. We all had trouble following the storyline, but when 150 shirtless male per-formers, all wearing identical checkered sarongs, started to sway and chant "Kecak" as if in a nighttime trance, we were taken by the rhythm. The primeval chant sounded as if the men were beating themselves into a frenzy to prepare for a special offering to the gods. When the few female dancers arrived resplendent in gold-and-red costumes, we were hooked.

When we returned home from the *Kecak*, Nava grew tear-ful. She was shaken by our visit to Nyoman's family compound and broke down in heaves. "I hate being rich in front of other people!" For all the relative privilege she enjoyed in New York, she had never felt different from others in such a stark way. I was glad she was aware of the different ways people live. Her tears spoke to feelings of guilt I had felt in New York, swaddled in the soft underbelly of Manhattan privilege.

"You know," I said, "a person's happiness has little to do with how much she actually has. Does Nyoman look unhappy to you?"

Nava sniffled.

"He has his family," I said, "and his community. Happiness is love. And one of the reasons we're here is because I love you and want to spend more time with you."

Nava calmed down, but while she understood the goals of our sabbatical, how long would my motivational speech divert her attention from the real inequity?

six 6

A sher stood at the coffee concession counter in the Green School *warung*. About fifty years old, he was thin, sported a graying goatee, and wore a tank top, baggy shorts, and a hipster straw hat over his long, curly hair. His mobile coffee roaster stood by his side. He happily engaged parents in any conversation, provided it had something to do with coffee or mountain biking. "I've been on a ten-year quest for the perfect cup of joe," he said. "I want to recapture the mystical and spiritual effects of coffee." He offered me a special brew of locally grown and freshly roasted coffee.

"I'm off coffee," I said. "Keeps me awake at night."

"C'mon, man. Coffee has powerful medicinal benefits. Plus, it'll be the best coffee you've ever tasted. Guaranteed."

"What the hell. I'm weak." The coffee was, as promised, magic in a cup.

Asher was the Green School dude, always ready with a Zen response, always at peace and the picture of equanimity. He was on a spiritual journey that started in New York and Connecticut. From the East Coast, he had moved to Oregon before making his way to Bali. Now in his early fifties, he was soaking in the magic of the local culture.

"Everything here is spiritual," he said. "The trees, the people, the food. Everything." I didn't really know what he meant, but I didn't dismiss him. I was open to taking in some of this. Having striven for success for so long, I was suddenly finding achievement to be empty and lonely. I'd never understood what *spiritual* meant outside the context of organized religion, which sometimes was more about observance than spirituality. And yet here was a man who seemed, at least on the surface, full of joy and love. I'd like some of that.

Asher also belonged to an entrepreneurial class that somehow had disappeared from the entrepreneurialism that I knew in the United States, where scale and disruptive innovation were everything. Whether it was technology businesses that could grow rapidly over a very short time period or consumer ideas that needed to be national or global to attract any attention, businesses had to dominate their sectors quickly in order to succeed. In Bali there was a kind of artisanal entrepreneurial spirit that was refreshing. Asher roasted and sold local coffee. Ben was a farmer who bought or leased land in order to bring organic food to the region. Charles built and sourced furniture to be sold in the United States and elsewhere. John Hardy designed, created, and sold jewelry. I was told that at one point, he was so successful that his company was the largest private employer in Bali.

Asher sipped a cup of his own brew. "Peter and I are going for a bike ride tomorrow afternoon. Want to join?" I didn't know what I was getting myself into but readily agreed. "We'll leave from here at four o'clock."

I showed up the next day with the locally constructed bike I'd bought. Asher had changed out of his baggy shorts into tight cycling gear. He introduced me to Peter, a Canadian entrepreneur and video journalist. He was a good decade younger than I and sported a soul patch of facial hair. Both Peter and Asher had slight bodies, but as we set out up an early hill, it was clear that their legs were powerful and their skill high. As we rolled along, I realized that whatever cycling skills I had picked up in New York on a road bike would be worthless in Bali on a mountain bike. Many of the roads were broken, and pathways often snaked alongside deep, lush ravines with no barriers to protect pedestrians and cyclists from plunging over the side.

The terrain was muddy from the rainfall earlier in the day. I struggled to control my bike around the quick turns and up sudden, sharp inclines. While Asher and Peter confidently zipped around, I was tentative and nervous. When they bounced down a set of stairs, I dismounted for fear of injury. While they practically floated on the trails, I plodded along cautiously.

Slowly, I gained confidence and picked up my pace. At one point, when we took a break to take in a view, a Balinese man asked if we would like some *kelapa muda*, a local drink made from fresh young coconut. He climbed a coconut tree and, with a small knife, picked the fruit and sliced off the top so that we could drink its water.

The light faded in the late afternoon. As we prepared to end our ride, Asher and Peter led me down a path along one of the canals in which the Balinese both bathed and disposed of their trash and sewage. In my peripheral vision, I spotted a young local woman washing in the canal. Just then, she stood up, exposing her topless torso. As my head spun around instinctively, my front wheel hit a dip in the track, and I sailed over the handlebars into the shallow canal water. When Peter and Asher backtracked to fish me out, I felt a deep pain in my right pinky finger. It was bent outward at a sharp right angle.

That evening, Nyoman took me to the closest medical clinic, in the town of Mas. The attending physician, using an X-ray machine as ancient as a Hindu god, bombarded my hand with radiation to determine that no bones were broken. To fix the severe dislocation, though, he needed to call in an orthopedist from Denpasar. An hour later, the specialist arrived on his motorcycle and waltzed in the front door. Without removing the bag from his shoulder, he stuck me with a long needle of anesthetic, then relocated my finger and told me to stay off my bike for a few days. Then he left the same way he came to rejoin the dinner date he said he'd abandoned at a restaurant table.

When I sheepishly told the kids what had happened, they all agreed I'd gotten what I deserved.

seven ༄

Two weeks later, I woke to a bright sun that laid down blocks of heat and air soupy with humidity. A motorbike was parked in the front of the house. "Five hundred thousand rupiah per month," Nyoman said, about fifty dollars. He had rented the bike for us from a friend and presented us with a gift: new bandanas he'd bought in the market to cover our noses and mouths as we traveled so we didn't have to suck in the clouds of exhaust from the traffic in front of us. The best way to get around the island was by motorbike, especially for short trips.

Victoria slung the strap of her yoga mat across her chest like a messenger bag and hopped onto the motorbike. "Hurry up, we'll be late!" I was busy with emails. "What happened to being present," she yelled, "to detaching? Get off that damn thing!" I gathered my belongings so fast, it was as if, like Shiva, I had four arms. I jumped on the back of the bike.

We motored toward Ubud and were immediately held up by a duck stampede, about one hundred strong, crossing the road and quacking up a racket. A farmer carrying a white flag on a bamboo pole herded them as they waddled their way from one rice field to the next. "Natural insecticide," Victoria said. Ducks ate bugs that damaged crops. "And fertilizer too."

When the ducks passed, we continued through the center of Ubud and down Hanuman Street, the main retail drag, named for the Hindu monkey god. We passed shops selling schlock art and T-shirts and past Kafe, a local hangout that attracted customers with organic food and free Wi-Fi. We turned left into the small alleyway that led to Yoga Barn and slotted our bike among the dozen others already parked. I noticed then that Nyoman had wedged a devotional offering tightly behind our front license plate. It might not quite provide the protection of a helmet, but I appreciated his gesture.

A schedule of classes was posted at the entrance of Yoga Barn, a smorgasbord of offerings ranging from power yoga to more esoteric practices like gong therapy and ecstatic dance. The moment I saw it, I knew why Yoga Barn billed itself as Southeast Asia's holistic healing and retreat center.

I didn't quite know what I was doing there. I had attempted yoga before and hated it. I found the practice hard, boring, and feminine. Resistance training and cardiovascular exercise were more my thing. Yoga was stretching, a necessary evil that came with real exercise. Plus, my body simply didn't move in the way yoga required. Even though every instructor I'd ever met had told me it was enough to simply do what I could, for me it was never enough. I wasn't wired for enough. If I was going to practice yoga, I was going to win at yoga.

Victoria paid the entrance fee for us both. We were just in time for the nine o'clock power yoga class, taught by Denise Payne, who stood at the front of the studio next to a four-foot elephant-head statue of the Hindu deity Ganesha. Out of the corner of my eye, I recognized a Green School parent preparing his mat and flashed him a smile. Denise was a yogi transplant from Arizona, but I could tell she'd been on a long journey of personal discovery before arriving in Bali. She was a single mom and attractive, and her body was a canvas for tattoo artists. She had a reputation for an aggressive teaching style. The class was scheduled to last nearly two hours.

As we got under way, Denise focused on physical strength, balance, and flexibility. She drew attention to the connection between the body and the earth, trying to ground her students both physically and emotionally. She began with the simplest of standing poses, mountain pose. "Feel the edges of your feet touch the earth," she said. I felt the heaviness of my body and the stiffness of my joints. The many weeks of travel had done nothing to increase my flexibility, strength, or endurance.

A pleasant breeze blew through the open space to cool my body as I grunted and strained my way through the poses. On her mat beside me, Victoria was having an easier time. She flowed from one pose to the next while I groaned. I tried to move my body the way Denise instructed, but it felt unnatural.

Heat began to build in my body as I pushed it from one awkward stance to the next. Barely thirty minutes into the session, I began to sweat, first lightly and then profusely. My yoga mat became so slick with the water dripping from my pores that my feet slipped and hands slid. I couldn't catch a grip. In desperation, I flipped my mat over to its dry side, and just in time too. We transitioned to poses that required my lying down on my belly.

I practically hoovered the floor with my heavy breathing. I arched my back, bent my knees, and reached back for my ankles. I couldn't find them. I tried again, wiggling my body to catch first my right ankle and then writhing to catch my left. Denise came over. "That's not the way. You need a little more grace. You have to catch both ankles at the same time." She made a small adjustment, and I barely managed to grab my ankles. After three breaths, my hands and ankles slipped apart.

I struggled through the rest of the class. In no time at all, another puddle developed on the reverse side of my mat. I was soaked, exhausted, and completely spent. I knew if I were going to make a go of yoga, I would have to get into better shape. When Denise instructed us to rest on our backs, I collapsed with arms and legs splayed like a butterfly. I closed my eyes, slowly steadied my breath, and drifted into a light sleep.

I woke to the sound of a single chime. Denise sat cross-legged at the front of the room, a candle and small bell by her side. She invited us to sit up tall in a meditative posture, placed her hands in a prayer position at her chest, and closed the practice with a traditional chant of *Om*. I looked over to Victoria, who smiled at me. We gathered our things and headed to the café next door.

Garden Café was typical of Ubud's spiritual culture. On the menu were vegan, vegetarian, organic, macrobiotic, and raw dishes along with Ayurvedic drinks, which the menu tagged as "Healing and transforming since 3,000 BC." We found a spot of shade, flopped onto the cushioned floor, and ordered a *kelapa muda*. When it arrived, I downed it in one shot. Victoria looked at me and said, "I could get used to this."

"If we keep coming to this class, I'm going to have to."

As my body recovered, my mind cleared. I felt fresh. Somehow focusing on my breath while moving through poses did make me feel grounded in the way Denise had promised. I recalled the names of the poses she had called out and how self-contradictory they sounded: devotional warrior, peaceful warrior, and humble warrior. To me, these names were not cynical in the way that, for example, naming a nuclear missile a "Peacekeeper" seemed to be. The names of the poses described a tension that spoke to me. They described a desire to aggress on the one hand and to pacify on the other.

I paid the check, ten thousand rupiah—about one dollar—and Victoria and I walked out. We passed by a community bulletin board just outside Yoga Barn. It was filled with flyers that promoted various healing arts: colonics, holistic medicine, acupuncture. One that struck me as particularly out of place advertised the services of a Cherokee medicine woman. Another that caught my eye was for Ashram Munivara, which advertised an evening introduction to meditation. Located near Tegalalang, a village only fifteen minutes from our home, it seemed just the thing.

Except that it also offered spiritual dance, fasting, and chanting designed to "enhance positive energy." That brought to mind images of the Beatles or Steve Jobs in their earlier days, when they explored spirituality. I had trouble taking it seriously. I thought of myself as rational and rigorous but nonetheless curious. Having struggled with tensions of work, sleeplessness, and self-criticism, I was open to a new approach. Meditation sounded promising. Wacky ashram or not, I needed to find out what it was all about. I was going to dive into Ubud's alternative culture.

As we motored home, I thought back to a moment, six months earlier, when I sat at the Lure Fishbar restaurant in SoHo wearing a fine wool suit and Italian shoes. The restaurant attracted an eclectic crowd, from entrepreneurs in New York's tech scene to well-heeled socialites and hipsters. Lure was designed and themed as the interior of a yacht and set in the semibasement of a converted factory. Its below-deck porthole windows, placed near the ceiling, opened to a view of the legs of hurried pedestrians on the sidewalk outside. From the inside looking out, the passing feet appeared as darting fish.

I was there early to meet Michael, an aggressive and successful litigator at a law firm known for its truculent tactics. We had a passing relationship that was mostly commercial. I had always known him to be a tough-minded professional despite his charming, self-deprecating sense of humor.

On the agenda for that day's meeting was an item that was anything but business as usual. Two weeks earlier, Take-Two had released a story to the press. It began, "Chief Executive Officer decides to step down in order to pursue plans to travel in Asia with his family for an extended period." Among the many reactions that I received from people outside the company, Michael's call was the most intriguing.

"Listen, I need to talk to you. I'll explain when I see you."

When Michael arrived, we talked for a little while about business and how things were progressing. I forked the brook trout on my plate with disinterest. My appetite had waned with the waxing tension at work.

"I was blown away when I read your announcement," Michael said.

"Why's that?"

He put on a shocked expression and threw his hands into the air. "Because nobody actually *does* it."

Again I speared the fish but left it on the plate.

Michael opened up to me in a way that I'd never expected from the kind of man I thought he was. He told me about the trade-offs he'd made in his career. "The thing I wanted to do when I was in college was to write. In some ways, I still want to be a writer."

"And?"

"Couldn't do it. I need to provide for my girls." Michael was married with two daughters. "The thing is, I grew up really poor. True poverty. There's no way I'm going to raise my kids with that kind of aching need." So Michael chose financial security and a genuine affection for the law as a greater calling. "I want to make enough money so my daughters never have to make the trade-offs I made."

"What's your number?" I asked, repeating the hackneyed MBA question of which I was growing weary. When he told me, it seemed to me so lofty a goal as to be a burden. Normally, I wouldn't have commented. But I wondered whether he was justifying to himself his pursuit of an activity that paid him more than he needed and was crowding out his true passion. Working hard for somebody else, especially your children, was an easy story to tell yourself.

"Are you sure you need that much?"

"Are you sure I don't?" He raised an eyebrow. "Are you sure you don't?"

What Michael did for a living wasn't who he was. That much was evident not just in his words but also in that he was willing to expose his vulnerability by reaching out to me. I recognized something of myself in Michael. We each had achieved success, had experienced the anxiety in our early lives of not having (though he more than I), and were somewhat surprised to find ourselves in abundant situations. And still we did not feel secure. We still felt the tension of not having and the worry about the future.

"So I quit my job," I said. "What do you do?"

"I meditate. Not as often as I'd like or as long, but I do what I can."

I always thought of meditation as something for escapists with too much time on their hands. "Does it help?"

"I think so. It helps me not get carried away with whatever crisis is brewing. I'm more centered and able to deal with whatever comes."

We spoke about meditation as a path to stilling the mind. I was struck then by the idea of making meditation a core goal of my sabbatical as a way both to recenter myself and to build up a practice that would help me live with the stress of work when I returned. But I never thought I'd have the patience for it. Like an addict, I craved distraction and stimulation. But soon I'd be one of those escapists with too much time on his hands.

The weekend after my lunch with Michael, I downloaded a book by Ellen Langer, a Harvard professor, who proposed a theory of what she called "mindfulness," which was the title of her book. Most of us, she postulated, have predictable responses to the stimuli in our environment. We follow routines and have automatic responses that can lead to wrong decisions, pain, and a "predetermined course of life." Our reactions tend to be automatically triggered by people and circumstance and are, in effect, unconscious choices. When we make these choices unconsciously, we are said to be mindless because it is as if we stumble through our days and years. When we make conscious choices, we are doing the opposite: being mindful and deliberate.

Mindfulness meditation, she wrote, is the practice of being aware of our surroundings, noticing the choices we make and the behaviors we adopt. Through meditation, we attempt to bring thoughts and behaviors from the periphery of our attention to the center. In that way, we take notice of our emotions and behaviors and witness them, as if from an observer perspective. The practice was derived from Buddhist meditation practice.

Mindfulness was already experiencing a boom in popular culture as men, women, and even children strived to cope with a hyperconnected world that, through the proliferation of electronics, constantly and persistently diverts their attention in many directions.

After reading Langer's book, I decided that one of my personal goals for my sabbatical would be to learn to meditate. Now as Victoria and I motorbiked into our driveway, I committed to giving it a try.

Also, as I had done a few times since coming to Bali, I phoned Take-Two just to check in, see how things were going. But I was clearly no longer in the loop.

The phone rang, but as usual, it was for Victoria. Her organization contacted her regularly. She tried to keep these calls away from the family as a disturbance to our sabbatical; it was a quiet house with no blaring media.

A key employee had threatened to quit, and Victoria was trying to turn her around. This evening, she learned she had failed. She hung up and slumped to the floor. "I just can't seem to get away."

∿

The following Tuesday, I left Victoria and the kids at the dinner table. Putu's mother had come by to prepare a Balinese dinner. The evening's cool air was just settling in, and the road was still wet from the rain shower that passed over earlier in the day. I set out by motorcycle and headed north on Jalan Tirta Tawar, the road that ran from Ubud, past our home, and through the rice fields toward the town of Tegalalang. I pulled down the visor on my helmet to protect my eyes from the midges that swirled, suspended in midair like miniature tornadoes. The road curved in long S patterns past the rice fields, villas, and the small village of Junjugan. Off to my right, I could see acres of the migrating herons for which Junjugan was known. To my left, a few rice farmers shuffled down the road after their day's work, sickles in hand, their sarongs filthy from the mud of the fields. I enjoyed the smooth shifting of my weight from side to side, as if I were slaloming down the pavement. I felt a tinge of excitement in anticipation of my first attempt at guided meditation at the ashram.

When I arrived at Ashram Munivara, the sky outside had faded to the pale lavender of dusk, and stars began to sprinkle the sky. I jacked the kickstand on my motorbike in the parking area. A stream of young women spoke softly to each other as they exited the ashram. I walked past them, through the arched entranceway of the compound, and descended the stepped pathway lined by coconut palms. The silence, the vast stillness of the place, settled around me. I passed a shrine and a housing pavilion and continued silently to the bottom, where the steps ended at a rushing river. Had I misjudged the time? Was I late?

Walking back up the pathway, I poked my head into the kitchen and found a man and woman sitting cross-legged on the floor eating their rice dinner. I asked about the class. The man motioned to meet him at the shrine just across the path. I removed my shoes at the entrance and put on a sarong that I had brought with me, local gestures of respect for the sanctity of the temple. I entered silently. A few minutes later, the man arrived with a cushion and sitar. There was no class; it was just him and me.

He asked me to sit on the cushion with my legs crossed and hands resting on my knees. I had thought sitting would be simple and straightforward. What could be more natural than planting my behind in a seat?

"Not that way," he said with a not-quite-Balinese accent that I couldn't place. "Keep your spine straight up, like an arrow." He gently held my wrists. "Like this, palms facing up. Relax your jaw and let your lips part slightly. Drop your shoulders. Close your eyes. That's it. Find your breath and feel it flow through your nose. Inhale and exhale slowly through your nose. There is nothing to think about, just be with your breath and watch your thoughts. When you feel your mind wandering, come back to your breath." When he judged that I was positioned correctly, he reached for his sitar. "If you have a religious experience while I play, please open your eyes and tell me."

I was with him until "religious experience." Something in me lit up, some emotion that lay between anger and skepticism. Religion was not what I was looking for and not what was advertised. My defenses flared. Had I wandered into a Hare Krishna den? The jaded New Yorker in me wondered if and when he would ask to be paid. At worst, I was being scammed, at best, misled.

But I stopped myself. Lately, when I felt cynical about a new experience, I tried to be open to it. In her landmark work on personal growth, *Mindset*, Stanford University's Carol Dweck explored why some people fulfill their potential while others don't. I had read the book following a leadership-training course in Colorado. Those who don't live up to their potential tend to believe their traits are fixed and new skills can't be learned beyond a certain age. She called that belief system a "fixed mindset" and found that it constrained development. On the other hand, those who believed they could develop new personality traits and even enhance their intelligence had what she called a "growth mindset," which freed them to pursue passionately what they valued. She discovered that what mattered most when it came to personal development was what people believed about themselves.

Now as I sat on the floor of an ashram, I told myself to be open-minded. I deliberately lowered my defenses and let fade whatever cultural assumptions I harbored. I sat there for about fifteen minutes with my eyes closed while he played, prepared to accept something wholly new.

Another English-speaking couple startled me by sticking their heads in the door and, oblivious to their surroundings, loudly asking for instruction on meditation. My guide ushered them into another room. He came back to play for two minutes more, then quickly packed up his stuff and left. At the very moment that I was ready to submit, ready to allow myself to be somewhat vulnerable, I was abandoned. I sat there alone, the daylight having completely surrendered to the dark of night, wondering what had happened.

I told myself my first foray into meditation was a failure. Confused, I rose and left. I strode back up the stepped pathway to my motorbike, fired it up, and headed toward our villa, more than a little annoyed.

On my way home, I thought about the guided meditation session and how it felt, well, misguided. I remembered some reading I'd done about brain science and specifically the brain's ability to reorient itself in response to experience. Not only does the brain shape thoughts; thoughts literally shape the brain. New skills and behavior patterns can be learned and cultivated, and meditation was one path to recalibrating neural networks. The old aphorism that people don't change was just plain wrong. I believed that if I could deliberately think certain thoughts through mental exercise, I could retune some neural pathways and the way my brain processed information—I could deliberately cultivate a less anxious and more compassionate way of being and gain a sense of ease and equanimity in the process.

I had reached a point in my life where I was not only open to change but actively seeking it.

In studies of the brain, I found a body of research supporting a philosophy developed by Buddhism—a 2,500-year-old tradition—that offered an entirely different approach from the one I had. For an investment as small as a few minutes of meditation per day, I might be able to achieve the peace of mind I was looking for.

And yet what had just happened at the ashram left a bad taste in my mouth. The expectation of having a "religious experience" was off-putting. The place seemed like a tourist trap, built for visitors to have a spiritual experience they could talk about when they returned home. I was looking for something deeper.

Once home, I took off my shoes, padded through the front door, and placed my helmet on the front table. Victoria gave me a quick backward glance from the sink where Nava was brushing her teeth before going to bed. "How was it?"

I shrugged my shoulders. "Not the epiphany I'd hoped for."

"Give it a chance."

"I know."

"Why don't you check out Yoga Barn?"

I opened their website, determined to continue exploring meditation to see if it could mollify my jumpy mind. The only meditation session they had on the schedule was a class called Tibetan Singing Bowl Meditation. I had just missed it, but there was a class every week.

It would have to wait, though, because we had planned a side trip. Green School, along with the rest of Indonesia, would be celebrating *Maulid Nabi Muhammad*, an Islamic holiday that marks the birth of the Prophet Muhammad. The weekend holiday coincided with the Chinese New Year, and we decided to head to nearby Singapore for a few days. I told Victoria I'd try meditation at Yoga Barn once we returned.

eight | ꙮ

The next week, the six of us boarded a Thursday flight on a low-cost Malaysian airline. We took our seats at the rear of the plane. As we taxied toward the runway, the pilot announced flight information on the public address system. He ended with the Muslim greeting "Salam" and then "May Allah bless our flight." Sam and Victoria glanced at each other with a puzzled look.

On the flight, Sam read about Singapore on his computer. He looked up with a mildly horrified look on his face. "This guy was once caned for overstaying his visa in Singapore. Caned!"

"And it's illegal to chew gum on the streets in Singapore," Victoria said. "How would you like to be caned for that?"

Nava frowned. "What's 'caned'?"

We had been in Bali only a few weeks but had already grown accustomed to the island's simple facilities and architecture. Singapore's glistening airport was anything but. The automatic toilets, sinks, and hand dryers in the men's room, once common to my boys, now seemed strangely luxurious. On the ride to the city from the airport, Oliver looked around in awe at the tall buildings as if he'd never lived in a city with skyscrapers. Just about every large building had a second-floor shopping mall with an escalator leading into it. The streets were paved straight and smooth, not the shoddy patchwork we had become accustomed to in Bali.

We checked into our hotel room and found a place to have a late Western-style breakfast. The kids had pancakes on their minds. As we took our seats, Oliver's jaw hung as he stared at the giant outdoor high-definition TV. A soccer match was under way. Victoria was shocked by the food prices, much higher than in New York, never mind Africa and Bali.

We walked around, taking in the sights. As we stood on a street corner, Rita said, "We can't stop here. It's illegal for six or more people to stand together without permission." We strolled around some more and, at lunchtime, took Singapore's immaculate subway to visit a kosher restaurant.

In our home, we ate only kosher food. The kids knew that access to nonvegetarian options while we traveled would be limited. Our plan was to make periodic trips to places like Singapore that had kosher meat and poultry, but we weren't certain. In any event, I had a backup plan.

〰️

The previous November, I traveled to the Mehadrin Kosher Poultry processing plant in Birdsboro, Pennsylvania. I brought along Seymour, a partner in my firm who, like me, ate only kosher food. As we arrived, three men greeted us. They sported long side curls, scraggly beards, and overgarments that bore specially knotted ritual fringes. These men were the shochets—religious Jewish men who were properly educated and trained in ritual slaughter. They had agreed to teach me to slaughter a chicken in accordance with Jewish law.

When Seymour and I arrived, two of the shochets invited us to join them for a chicken-farm breakfast of eggs and more eggs. That kind of breakfast seemed like overkill, considering why we were there. We passed.

They led us to the processing facility, which was being scrubbed and prepped for the day's work. The lifeblood of the assembly line was a stainless-steel overhead conveyor system that snaked around the plant, above a concrete floor, passing from one workstation to the next. I had expected to be disgusted by the facility. Instead, I was impressed. The place was immaculate.

The shochets led us to a room at the back of the facility. One of them launched into a crash course on both Jewish and US Department of Agriculture rules and regulations. "Most importantly," he said, "the chickens must be killed with compassion and respect." He demonstrated how to hold the knife and the bird. When I had the basics down, we headed to the plant floor.

One shochet stood with me, the other with Seymour. A third observed the other two. The one who worked with me stood at the head of the assembly line and checked his blade. The conveyor belt started up with a whir and a jerk. A worker arrived with the first crate of live chickens. Four assistants stood by.

One assistant worker picked up a chicken from its crate and handed it to two other workers, who grabbed it by its wings, flipped it on its back, and held it still. Moving quickly, the shochet pinched the chicken's nape with his left hand to clearly expose the neck. He held his straightedge blade between the thumb and index finger of his right hand and, in one stroke, sliced swiftly. Blood spurted out. With his left thumb, he flicked back the head to ensure that the esophagus, carotid arteries, and windpipe were all clearly severed.

The fourth worker then grabbed the dead chicken and attached it by its legs, head down, to the overhead conveyor system. Away the bird went, quickly moving along the conveyor system from one automated station to the next, each mechanically executing a single element of the food-creation process: defeathering, gutting, salting, and packaging. A small channel in the floor caught and carried away the blood that continued to drain.

To inspect the birds, a shochet sat at a station next to an inspector from the USDA. The shochet checked first for quality as regulated by Jewish law, then the USDA inspected for quality according to federal regulation. Any chicken that did not meet requirements was removed and discarded. All told, the three shochets put ninety chickens per minute on that assembly line. It was fast, clean, and nearly fully automated.

Then my guy turned to me. "Ready?"

I definitely was not ready, but I stepped forward. I tried to mimic his movements but was too tentative. "Don't hold the chicken like that. Like this." He firmly grabbed the back collar. With him next to me, I took the knife and slit that poor chicken's throat. Like slicing through butter, the sharp blade slid effortlessly across and through the chicken's flesh. The blood was as fire-engine red as my own.

I killed two more chickens and stepped aside with no interest in slaughtering any more. While I felt the power of taking a life, I took no joy in it. Taking an animal's life might be morally sound if it was for food, but because I wasn't licensed, the animal needed to be removed from the production line and discarded. It was wasted, and I was not okay with that.

I realized how far removed I was from the very basics of my own food's preparation—that a bird available and packaged beautifully at a local supermarket was at some point slaughtered, defeathered, and trimmed by specially trained professionals. While I didn't enjoy the experience of killing a chicken, knowing firsthand where my food, or at least my chicken, had come from and how it arrived at my table made me understand more about local food and the growing local-food movement in the United States.

My guy pulled me aside. He gave me two items as gifts: a *chalef*, the razor-sharp knife for ritual slaughtering, and a book outlining the rules and regulations associated with ritual slaughter. Then he made an observation. True training required a lot more than half a day in a slaughterhouse. "If you're serious about this," he said, "have somebody else do it."

〰︎

I thought about using that *chalef*, which I had packed carefully and carried with me to Bali, when my kids were having a tough time adjusting to Indonesian food. After all, in Bali, chickens were ubiquitous. They clucked and strutted along our street and flew to the sides as my motorcycle sped past. Some of Bali's roosters were hardened killing machines in the local cockfights, which were illegal and dangerous but nonetheless easy to find. I was confident I could take down one of those birds and do the grisly work necessary to put it in a pot. But I didn't know if the connection between the bird on the road and the food on the table would be too obvious for my children to stomach. Now that we were in Singapore, though, the urgency had abated, at least for the time being.

Lunch at the restaurant on Waterloo Street would be the kids' first taste of meat or poultry in over a month, but Nava grew grumpy. She loved animals and cried upon hearing the reason that Nyoman was fattening up the pig in his compound. She hated that people killed and ate animals. Ever since Africa, she had been on what she called, in her seven-year-old way, "extra human offense, extra animal defense." That's how she now referred to people—the "humans."

As we sat to eat, she put her head down and fumed through her nose, pretending she was a dragon expressing her anger. In an impetuous tone, she announced that a Chinese girl in school was no longer her friend because the girl wanted the kitchen staff to cook her a grasshopper. Nava clearly wasn't planning on eating the chicken nuggets we'd ordered. Before either Victoria or I could say anything, Sam started talking to her, somehow connecting to her childlike logic and convincing her that the chicken had, in a dignified way, committed suicide. She began to eat.

Sam had become very tuned in. Back in New York, he barely spoke to his youngest sister, not because he thought she was inferior or unimportant, but because he was so caught up in his own thoughts and needs. Now he was changing. He developed an easy sense of humor. And he used it, as he just had, to connect with the rest of the family in a new way.

The other kids wolfed down as much as they could. Even though the vegetarian food in Green School had been fresh, tasty, and abundant, they had been tempted by the smells of forbidden dishes that wafted from the school's kitchen. Sam began to reminisce about meals back home, where it was easy to obtain kosher meat and poultry. Then he shoved three more nuggets and two hot dogs down his gullet.

I had no interest in the food. My mind was elsewhere. Singapore, even in the midst of the Chinese New Year holiday, was a busy, dynamic city, a global financial and business center. Simply being around the distractions of big-city life brought my mind back to my career. It was February, and I still had not quite disengaged. Part of me fantasized about being back in the thick of things. I ruminated about my decision to take myself out of the game and how it might affect my career, for a while or forever. As I reflected, I noticed what I was doing and wanted to stop. I was dwelling on the past, which in addition to not serving me was working against me. But in that business hive, I felt powerless against the impulse. As if I needed a reminder, I recommitted to finding a different way to deal with my inner monologue. I made a mental note to attempt meditation again.

༄

I emailed Hubert, Take-Two's Asia regional director, who was based in Singapore, and asked him to coffee. He must have been surprised to hear from me but readily agreed. As he and I sat in the lobby of the Hyatt hotel, I avoided confidential topics or those that would be difficult or inappropriate for him to talk about. We spoke for nearly two hours while Victoria took the kids for breakfast and wandered around downtown. Somehow Oliver convinced her to return to the pancake restaurant, his interest in watching sports on the big screen trumping her horror at the prices.

I asked Hubert about projects we'd worked on together, about coworkers, and more generally about developments in the video game business. It was a huge industry undergoing a lot of change and replete with strategic issues, challenges, and opportunities. It surprised me how much I was still interested in the operations of the company. He too seemed puzzled and finally asked if I regretted having left.

Left? I had left Take-Two but had seen my time away as a sabbatical rather than a departure. I shared some of what I had been thinking when I stepped down, that I needed a break and that the pursuit of success—the burning desire to reach ever higher—had, at least for the moment, broken down for me. There was always something more to accomplish or more success to be had. I couldn't quite articulate it, and I wasn't sure he understood what I said, although he said he did, even if he didn't see things the same way.

When the waiter brought the check, Hubert picked it up. As I walked out, I felt amped up by talking business amid a big city with its noise and energy, but it quickly faded with the realization that it was vicarious. I was now an outsider looking in.

I rejoined my family in our hotel lobby, and we set out to tour the city. Cars and trucks sped past in a fury as we walked to Chinatown and Little India. We bought a printer and other provisions we couldn't easily find in Bali. Shopping for computer supplies in that bustling electronics store was far from the sanctuary I sought. After only a few weeks in Bali, away from any commercial hubbub, all of a sudden I was back in the thick of things.

That Sunday, we boarded our flight at four thirty in the afternoon and returned via the same route. I used the travel time to read, soaking in more information on meditation and the brain science behind it, still taken by the idea that thoughts shape the brain as much as the brain shapes thoughts.

As we prepared for our descent, the pilot got on the PA and asked passengers to fasten their seat belts. And then: "Ladies and gentlemen, the possession and trafficking of drugs are serious offenses in Indonesia and carry the death penalty. Don't get involved." Sam gave me an odd look and then laughed. It was a shocking thing to hear. I thought a few people might get up to use the toilet at that point, but everyone stayed in their seats. I guessed they knew the drill.

By the time we landed, we were ready to be back in Bali. Oliver said that Singapore was cool for a while, but he really just wanted to get back to Ubud, where everything was green, small, and inexpensive; where roads, architecture, and merchandise were not so straight-edged, linear, and shiny; where he didn't have to get up early and wander around a strange city.

I knew how he felt. I was happy to be back too.

nine ꙍ

More than one month since we had arrived in Bali, we began to settle into a daily routine. At seven thirty each morning, Victoria woke the girls, and I rousted the boys by opening the blinds and plucking the earplugs from Sam's ears. When they opened their eyes, they could see, through the glass door, Nyoman in his sarong, roaming the yard, placing offerings and lighting incense.

We ate breakfast outdoors, typically freshly cut fruit and yogurt. Sometimes we Skyped with family back home, taking advantage of the brief window the thirteen-hour time difference afforded us. When we were done, Nyoman drove the kids to school. Sometimes we joined them, but not always. There were days when we just waited for the ants to arrive. Full battalions showed up to remove any crumbs from the patio. If the take was large, reinforcements arrived. Their columns often stretched from one end of the property to the other. They didn't mess with us, and we returned the courtesy.

Victoria and I spent an hour or so catching up on emails and generally taking care of business. I had anticipated a steady if dwindling number of emails and calls from Take-Two and my partners and was at first relieved there were so few. Then I began to miss the connection and even feel alarmed that they had adapted so quickly to functioning without me.

Victoria was still getting a lot of emails and calls from her former organization. I joked one day that this was supposed to be her sabbatical too.

She smiled. "But mainly yours."

For a second or two, I tried to brew up a bantering come-back, until her meaning washed over me and spun my perspective around to a new and humbling angle. Although we had discussed our uprooting as a family adventure, I had been the one most in need of a break. I had to be fixed before any other remedies could bite.

Most mornings, after checking emails, we motorbiked down to Denise's yoga class. In time, my yoga practice improved. My flexibility, strength, and balance developed. I easily centered on my breath and found myself in that concentration. I focused on the four corners of each of my feet touching and pressing into the mat. In warrior poses, I felt the strength and the solidity of my body as if it was an immovable object prepared and willing to stand fast against any force. For long breaths at a time, I held my ground.

Sometimes, I looked over at Victoria. For her, yoga was a way to keep fit and healthy rather than a spiritual or even religious practice. But it was becoming something more for me as the tension that had built up over the years slowly seeped out of me like groundwater. I wondered where else it might take me.

We ate two-dollar lunches in town, sometimes with friends from Green School, other times alone. We strolled the art galleries and museums or simply returned to the villa to read before it was time to pick up the kids from school.

Ben's Organic Farm made home deliveries, and Putu's mother joined her daughter periodically to prepare Balinese dishes for dinner. She made *gado gado*, a salad of slightly boiled or steamed vegetables and hard-boiled eggs served with a peanut dressing;

nasi campur, white rice with small portions of vegetables and coconut fritters; and *nasi goreng*, simple fried rice.

Most evenings we read, watched a movie, or played board games. By ten o'clock, it was lights out.

I had underappreciated how much time Victoria and I would spend together on sabbatical. Stripped of our New York trappings and the pressures of home and work, there was no place for me to hide. We shared every meal and almost every activity. Sometimes we got frustrated with each other, and it was not always pretty. But we knew we'd made brave decisions and conquered our beyond-this-point-there-be-dragons mentality. We had made a deliberate choice to take time out to invest in our relationships and ourselves. Together, we were committed to pushing the frontier of experience.

∿

One evening, I made my way to Yoga Barn for their evening Tibetan Singing Bowl Meditation class. I arrived ten minutes early to secure a spot, removed my shoes, and walked into the same studio in which Victoria and I practiced power yoga. Instead of Denise standing in the front of the room, Swami Arun sat there cross-legged and dressed entirely in white. His hair was a Medusa's tangle of long dreadlocks tied at the crown of his head so that they sprouted like a large shock of crabgrass. In a semicircle before him, he placed about a dozen metallic bowls of various sizes.

Arun asked the participants to grab yoga mats and lie on their backs in a semicircle in front of him, heads toward the center. He picked up a mallet in each hand and tapped either side of the bowls, creating a soft gong-like sound. Then he repeated that for the other bowls, producing a symphony of reverberating gongs. By rubbing the mallet around the outside edge of the rim of the bowl, he created a high-pitched harmonic sound. Arun stood, holding a small cushion in his hands, on top of which he placed a midsized bowl. He brought the singing bowl around the room. When he came to me, he placed it first next to my right ear and then the left.

There was no particular melody to the sounds of the bowls, but I found them deeply relaxing. Arun asked us to close our eyes as he continued to work the singing bowls, creating a symphony of vibration, an invitation to let go of my thoughts and succumb to relaxation. I remembered the instruction I had received at the ashram and tried to be aware of my thoughts, tried to watch them, almost clinically, as if they were secretions of my mind. But the room was dark, I was lying flat on my back, and Arun's voice was too soothing. Within minutes, I was fast asleep.

I awoke after about twenty minutes to the sound of a large gong. The other people in the class had fallen asleep too and were now stirring. I pushed myself up from the floor, crossed my legs, and sat a few minutes longer. Then I bowed my head as instructed and stumbled out of the room in a semislumber.

On my motorbike headed home, I grew concerned that meditation in Bali was inaccessible for someone like me. Where was the peace of meditation without the weirdness? Where was I supposed to connect with the wisdom of meditation without succumbing to swamis, ashrams, and religious experiences?

By the time I powered down my bike in front of our home, I abandoned the idea of taking classes or learning from a teacher. Instead, I decided to turn to established experts. That approach had seemed to work for me many times before both personally and professionally. Thankfully and ironically, they were easily available on one of those electronic devices from which I had sought sanctuary, the Kindle.

Our home was one of the lucky few with a consistent if slow Wi-Fi connection, and I downloaded volume after volume, looking for pointers on various meditation practices. The first was the most impactful. *Joyful Wisdom* was written by a Buddhist monk with a light touch and a sense of humor. He'd been born with what would later be labeled severe anxiety disorder, which he overcame through meditation. I went on to read everything by Jon Kabat-Zinn, Dan Siegel, and Richard Davidson. Sitting uncomfortably cross-legged on cushions, I listened to guided meditation podcasts by Joseph Goldstein and Sharon Salzberg.

Through research, I learned that mindfulness meditation was not prayer. There was no deity, no praise, honor, or supplication. There was neither asking for help nor seeking answers. Meditation was prayer's opposite. It taught the practitioner simply to be, without praise or judgment.

Nor was meditation relaxing in the way that, for example, a massage was relaxing. Meditation required concentration. It required an upright spine and alertness. Letting the mind drift off in a relaxed state defeated the purpose. And yet, as a result of focused attention, the end of a meditation practice resulted in a refreshed sensation.

I learned that to sit in silence alone with my thoughts was to observe them dispassionately and nonreactively. As thoughts came and went, there was an infinitesimal moment between them, like the space between frames in an old movie reel or the frames in a graphic novel. That empty, miniscule instant between one thought and the next was a tiny, quiet moment of peace. My aim was to stretch that empty space, to slow down transitions of thoughts so that the in-between bits were more pronounced, less like the space between fast-moving movie frames and more like the turning of a page in a book. The goal of meditation was not to empty my mind of thoughts—that would be impossible— but to be so aware of them that I could experience fully the space between them. It was a gigantic goal, and I accepted that it was likely to be an aspirational one that could easily be pursued over a lifetime.

I learned too that in meditation, as in many other situations, failure is unavoidable. While the basic technique of meditation is focusing attention on the breath, inevitably attention wanders to any number of distractions. And when it does, attention breaks down. In that way, meditation was an exercise in failure.

But failure fed recovery, and the recovery in meditation was both easy and constructive. The critical moment came in the instant of recognizing the wandering mind and bringing attention back to the breath and refocusing. Meditation was a cycle of losing and regaining attention, of failure and recovery.

In one of my early sessions, I learned a lesson for the businessperson, more than just the old saw that failure is part of the process. Thoughts of past failures and missed goals kept intruding into my mind. I got caught up in the first two or three digressions but was able to quickly refocus on my breath, and I felt stronger. I realized, without dwelling in it, that each of those "failures" had led to recovery and each recovery to strength. Later I read that Dweck, the Stanford psychologist, had discovered that the entrepreneur or professional who does not accept failure as an inevitable outcome of trying and learning, who adopts an attitude of judgment and criticism or labels career experiences as either failures or successes, is less likely to recover, develop, and grow. For that person, failure is an unacceptable outcome from which recovery is not a learning experience. Failure is a sin from which redemption can only be wrought through yet more success. Whether failure translates to a growth experience often depends on one's frame of mind.

I thought back to my decision to take a break from my career and how concerned I was that some might have construed it as failure. I needed to remind myself that I had voluntarily walked away from my job and possibly from some close relationships that were deeply important to me. In meditation, I cultivated a mindset that did not require my attachment to success. I needed to do the hard work of changing the wiring of my mind, of noticing when I felt like a failure and shifting my thoughts, if only slightly, to construct a different narrative, one that included a sense of growth, discovery, and new experience.

An underlying aspect of meditation gradually became more and more clear to me. It's a practice, not a single event. My experience at the ashram was set up to fail. It was impossible to have a meaningful experience, religious or otherwise, simply sitting with eyes closed, listening to a man in a sarong playing the sitar. What was required was a dedication to sit daily, if only for a few minutes, with the intention of being still with my thoughts. It could take years of daily practice for meditation to have its effect. The brain does not change overnight. The investment in meditation was not a few minutes. It was a few minutes each day for many, many days over months and years. Meditation was like an insurance policy, small premiums paid regularly over a long time that brought both a little peace of mind and, in the event of a crisis, a lot of help, even salvation.

I started a daily practice. It was a struggle, but I kept it up. Someday, I thought, I might need to harvest my investment.

〰️

One afternoon, a few weeks after the Tibetan singing bowl session, I waited at the Green School *warung* to pick up my kids. John Hardy was giving another one of his campus tours with Ben McCrory at his side. He was walking past the *mepantigan*, a large mud pit where the school staged a monthly local martial arts performance of fire, dance, and drama set to gamelan music. "We take a mud-between-the-toes approach to education. Creativity here is as important as literacy."

There were times at Green School when creativity seemed *more* important than literacy, to say nothing of math and science. Still, I was impressed by John. He was like other people I knew who were brilliant but, because they couldn't perform well at school or had a learning disability, believed they weren't. Here was a man who had clear talent and vision yet had to find workaround strategies for traditional success.

I surmised that by developing Green School, John was attempting to heal his own childhood experience of suffering at the hands of an uncaring and ignorant educational system. He built the school he wished he'd attended. Green School's struggle with its curriculum reflected its founder's early struggle with core subjects. Still, John's inner call for social justice, with a particular focus on environmental awareness and the impact of humans on the planet and its resources, was impressive. "When my grandchildren ask me what I did about the planet we're destroying, I want to have a good answer," he once said.

John excused himself, turned the tour over to Ben to continue, and headed my way. With a hand on my shoulder, he led me away from the others. "Ben, I'd love to have you on our board of directors."

Before he could say another word, I stopped and shook my head. "I'm flattered, but no, thanks. I've just pulled myself away from all that."

He seemed a little taken aback by my knee-jerk response, and so was I.

"I hope you won't mind if I ask you again in a couple of months."

I laughed, mostly to ease the awkwardness. "Sure. Who knows?"

"Now I have an offer you can't refuse. A bunch of us are going on a mountain-bike trip to Java. It would be great if you could join." At sixty-one, John was a strong cyclist. He was heavy, but his legs were powerful. On local outings of the Green School Cycling Club, he was always at the head of the pack.

I had mixed feelings about leaving my family during a time I'd committed to spending with them. Still, I felt the pull of getting to know John better as well as the other parents of the Green School community. And spending a few days of exercise outdoors on a mountain bike held strong appeal. But John was the major draw. He was a highly creative force; if anyone else had asked, I would have declined on the spot.

John was working with another Green School parent, Jon, to arrange accommodations, travel, and transportation of our bikes. Peter, the Canadian journalist, would take videos with his GoPro helmet cam. John and Jon had hired two local guides to help us navigate our way from our start in Lake Bedugul, a mountain vacation spot about an hour's drive north of Ubud; to the Ijen volcano complex in West Java; then on toward the city of Malang; and finally to Surabaya to catch a flight home.

For all my talk about family time, I wasn't sure why I was so tempted to go on this trip. Since there was no way to bring the kids along, it would mean I'd be away from them and Victoria for a few days. Life after sabbatical would likely involve as much business travel as before, and I remembered all those awkward times I'd approached Victoria and my children with, "I need to travel; I'm not going to be home for a few days." Those conversations were tough even as they became routine. It hurt me to see disappointment in Victoria's eyes.

After dinner, I pulled Victoria aside. The kids were working on a thousand-piece jigsaw puzzle of the Sydney Opera House that we had bought in Singapore. I explained about the bike trip. "What do you think?"

She gave me that sigh I used to get when I told her I'd be away on business. She had left a professional career when Rita was born, surrendering to the realization that she could not do or have it all—career, husband, kids, the home. My trips reminded her that she was the mom while I was the traveler, and it was a sore point. Each time I told her about an upcoming trip, I felt I was slipping a stiletto between her ribs, and I braced myself for a quick spark of resentment. I felt guilty for forcing her inner conflict to the fore.

"Really?" she now said. She checked her calendar for any potential conflicts. There were none. Suddenly, her expression recovered, and she seemed wide open to the idea. "It's your sabbatical. Enjoy it. I'll go cycling with the ladies here."

"When's your turn?" I said.

She laughed. "Don't worry 'bout it. I'm doing my thing."

When I told my kids, they didn't seem to care. I was surprised, but perhaps I shouldn't have been. Far from being offended, I took it as a good sign of their growing self-confidence. Maybe things weren't so fraught after all. Maybe I was able to prioritize my wants without worrying about my sense of responsibility or loyalty to others. The trip was a month away. I decided to go.

ten ꠸ꠧ

I t was late February, a time of year when I would normally be fighting the doldrums of winter's short days and long shadows. Now I was counting my blessings. One morning, I realized that it had been many days since I'd caught myself chewing over past or hypothetical work concerns. A few weeks earlier, in Singapore, I'd noticed a softening of my avid attention on business. Now I'd finally stopped dwelling on my career and work life. With those tensions melting away, the cobwebs were clearing from my mind. I slept through most nights. During the day, my concerns were closer to home.

I was uneasy about Nava. Of all our kids, she was the one who most missed her friends and teachers in New York. She cried so often about returning home. "What if we had a Skype session with your classmates back home?" Victoria asked one night. Nava nodded through tears and agreed.

Rita had joined the school basketball team, where she discovered a welcoming and high-spirited group of girls. She had playdates and sleepovers. She still sometimes fought with Oliver, but mostly she returned home from school smiling. When she felt blue, I took her into town for some father-daughter time, which both calmed her and fed me. At bedtime one evening,

Rita said, "The kids are really nice here. I think I'm going to like it." I thought I saw a tear in Victoria's eye.

∿

One night, Victoria was on her computer answering emails. "Are Eric and Sharon coming for a visit with their family?"

I had been back and forth with our Chicago friends trying to fix a date for them to visit with their three kids. "I just locked it down today. April. My brother and his family are thinking of joining us for Passover too."

"Pak Chris wants to know if Oliver could participate in Sea to Summit." Being in Bali hadn't completely liberated us from logistics and planning. Oliver's science teacher, Chris, was known to students by the Indonesian honorific *Pak*, or sir. He was planning a four-day experiential field trip that would leave in April to study the interrelated ecologies of stream, reef, and mangrove in the north of the island. It sounded exciting, but Oliver hadn't quite jelled with his classmates. Victoria said she wasn't comfortable sending him off that long with faculty she barely knew. She wrote back to ask for some time to decide.

I walked to Oliver's room and heard a symphony of crickets outside, tweeting as if rhyming with the chirping geckos in the house. The geckos lived on the tall ceiling of our home and were impossible to remove. But they left us alone, preferring to keep their distance and hunt for mosquitoes.

Oliver was on his bed with a night-light, reading one of the volumes from Rick Riordan's *Heroes of Olympus* series. I brought my own book, downloaded to my Kindle, Daniel Pink's *A Whole New Mind*. I wanted to be with Oliver, not on a computer communicating with a virtual person elsewhere on the planet. I wanted to be present. I asked Oliver if I could join him. He gave me a preteen half nod. "Sure." I lay down next to him and turned on my Kindle.

Pink argued that the working skills required of Oliver's generation were going to be vastly different from those of my
generation. The economic power of computer automation would
only increase, and the costs of outsourcing would only decrease.
Anything that could be outsourced or automated would be. That
included jobs I'd considered to be the domain of highly educated
knowledge workers. He predicted that the technical professions
my generation was encouraged to enter—law, medicine, and
finance, for example—were going to see dramatically reduced
monetary rewards. In fact, they were already experiencing it.
Getting a good education was no longer a guarantee of anything. On the other hand, careers that involved creativity, innovation, and new ideas—like developing new products, brands,
and services—were going to be important, as were those that
required a physical human touch.

Careers that required an interdisciplinary approach also
would be critical. He put forth a concept of "symphony,"
an aptitude he described as the ability to pull together dispa-
rate pieces of a puzzle to find a solution. It was the talent to
synthesize and observe the relationships and patterns among
unrelated areas, to invent new things by connecting seemingly unrelated dots. Being able to find the right answers to questions was
unimportant.

Drawing, Pink wrote, was a terrific way to develop the
aptitude of symphony. As an example, Pink referenced Betty
Edwards's *Drawing on the Right Side of the Brain*, written almost
thirty years earlier. She held out the promise that she could
teach anybody to draw. "Drawing is not really very difficult,"
she wrote. "Seeing is the problem." And the secret to seeing is
quieting the left side of the brain so that the right side is free to
explore and express.

Here was the concept of neuroplasticity, written in 1979
language, well before the subject became popular, well before
functional MRI machines mapped the activity of the human
brain, and well before Dweck had written about open mindsets,

personal growth, and the ability to take on new skills. When Edwards was first published, the understanding of how the brain worked was elementary compared to what has been learned since. Nonetheless, I took in what she had to say. She used as her starting point the notion that the left side of the brain was verbal and rational, while the right side was nonverbal and intuitive. The left side thinks serially and reduces its thoughts to numbers, letters, and words. The right side thinks in patterns or pictures that are composed of whole things. It does not comprehend reductions like numbers, letters, or words but thinks in a way consistent with Pink's notion of symphony.

Edwards described the process of learning to see as an artist as shifting from "L-Mode" to "R-Mode." To me, her language reflected a naïve view of the brain because it implicitly used the metaphor of the brain as a computer. Our brains don't really have modes, and neuroscience has since moved beyond notions of left and right sides that mimicked the physical features of the human brain, but I understood it was a simple way to get her point across. Through a series of exercises designed to set free R-Mode thinking, she promised to teach just about anybody to draw by learning to see like an artist.

I glanced over at Oliver. His eyes were beginning to droop. I gave him a brief hug, which he neither returned nor fought. I tiptoed out and glanced at the sequins of stars, so unfamiliar to me not because the view in the Southern Hemisphere is unlike the Northern but because the light pollution of the big city obliterated any view at all.

I thought about whether the benefits of this sabbatical for my kids would outweigh any downside and had occasional concerns over whether pulling them out of a traditional school environment might cause them to lose ground compared to their classmates. But Pink argued—and Edwards would have too—that removing them from their routine patterns of learning and exposing them to entirely different cultures and schools of thought would make their thinking more open and flexible, more interdisciplinary in their approach—in other words, more in line with Pink's symphony. Bringing them to Bali might actually open them to more learning and new possibilities.

Nor was youth a necessary condition for thinking in new ways. Langer would have argued that the brain was much more flexible than Edwards imagined. If my children could learn to think in new ways, so could I. Over the years, through practice and discipline, I had honed a rational and analytical way of thinking. I was as far as anyone could get from a creative artist. So I decided to use Edwards's book to put to the test the hypothesis that even someone like me could learn to draw. I would discover for myself how flexible the brain really was. Was it really never too late to learn a new skill?

I downloaded Edwards's exercises. The first was to record the baseline of my drawing skills by drafting three sketches: a self-portrait, a portrait from memory of someone I knew, and my left hand drawn with my right hand. When I was done, I reviewed my work.

All three were worse than awful. To the extent that my self-portrait looked like a human being at all, it was of an obese man twice my age. My left hand looked like a mangled gecko that had been run over on Ubud's main road. The portrait from memory was nothing I would dare show anyone. Despite my horror at what I produced, I thought again of Dweck's work and reminded myself not to be self-critical. The point here was not to prove to myself that I was talented but to learn and to test the ability of my mind to acquire a new skill.

Following Edwards's next set of instructions, I laid out on the table a copy of a simple line drawing by Picasso. With nothing but a pencil and paper, I tried to re-create Picasso's work in freehand. The result of that drawing was as dreadful as my previous three.

The next instruction was again to reproduce Picasso's line drawing, only this time upside down so that the subject's feet were at the top of the page and his head at the bottom. I drew it that way, upside down, and when I finished the exercise, I flipped my page upright.

I was astounded. While it was far from perfect, my drawing was a reasonable replica of the original. I was in awe. I questioned what had happened in the way one questions a magic trick: What was the catch?

It turned out that copying an inverted drawing diminished my ability to discern features like a nose or a foot and label them in my mind—*Oh, that's a nose, that's a foot.* Instead, I thought in terms of lines, angles, and shapes. I thought too about the relationships among them and how they fit together. It made sense to me that if I'd labeled a body part—an eye, for example—I would have tapped into my fixed notions of what an eye should look like instead of observing, in an open and curious way, the shape, lines, and angles of this particular eye and how those features related to one another. Drawing a portrait wasn't about some innate ability to draw. It was about observation and awareness. In that way, it was a close cousin to mindfulness meditation.

I was blown away by the discovery of what I could do. I went on to the next exercise and then the next. Over the next two weeks, I completed Edwards's course, learning about perspective, foreshortening, light, and shadow. I looked not only at what was in front of me but also what was not, the negative space—the space around and between elements of a subject, like the space between two legs.

In art, as in meditation, the space between things was as important as the space they occupied, much in the way that, in personal relationships, what was not said was often more important than what was. Focusing on that in-between space in art clarified subjects just as it elucidated thoughts and emotions in meditation. My challenge was to focus on what was real and discard what was imagined. When that happened, paradoxes emerged that had me questioning the truth of what I was seeing. For example, when taking in the three-dimensional world and committing it to two dimensions on paper, lines that I perceived as horizontal really weren't. Parallel lines appeared to converge. There was more to learn from trying to draw the corner of a ceiling than I could have ever imagined.

My set notion of what *I was expecting to see was at odds with what was actually in front of me.* It was almost as if what I saw was an illusion, a construct of my mind. That made sense to me: although I had two eyes, two lenses, and two optical nerves, I perceived only a single image, not two, and that had to be at least in part an illusion that my mind created. We see with our brains, not our eyes.

Over time, as I continued to draw, I perceived things that had been in front of my face my entire life but had not quite registered. I had never been concerned with light and shadow before. I'd never comprehended the world around me as shapes, lines, and edges. My mind simply processed the information quickly so that I inherently knew, for example, that a shadow on the left side of an object implied a light source to the right. My mind unconsciously and instantly filled in that information.

One day, sitting outside in our garden, I held up my two thumbs and forefingers to form a rectangle. Sam walked by just then and said, "Drawing again?" I was getting used to his wisecracks.

I was framing the view of a nearby plant. "If you look at the scene through your fingers, you can visualize the composition more easily." Its large green teardrop leaves pointed in all directions, some straight and vertical, others folded or twisted in a tyranny of complexity. A gentle breeze blew, and I froze with the stunning realization that seeing the way an artist sees also means capturing stillness in objects that move. I made an ambiguous connection to creating my own stillness by moving to Bali.

Learning to draw was learning to understand. I surrendered to the reality of what I was seeing. I discovered firsthand what neuroscientists now know: that our senses give us only limited information, and our brains fill in the gaps to create a whole, coherent, and somewhat distorted sensation or image, often with emotions now attached. We invent things all the time. We invent the stories of our lives to fit what we think *should be* in order to make sense of things that in fact are incomprehensible. That insight aligned with the Buddhist philosophical idea that the self is an illusion, a construct of our own minds.

On another day, sketching in the garden, I noticed how the color green changes hue over the course of a day, how it varies as the wind blows, how it differs from the bottom of a leaf to the top. Accepting the illusion of sight somehow opened my sense of perception and awareness. In a way, the brain creates a certain deception, a fiction to make a scene quickly graspable to the conscious mind. To capture the differences, I began mixing colors, adding brown to the green to capture shade. When I pulled out a pencil to draw the flowers, I noticed how the wonderful red hue of the flowers plays against the green of the leaves. Red and green simply go together naturally, like tomatoes and basil.

To see as an artist sees was to accept the world as it is. I knew many people who wanted their lives to be different from those they were actually leading, unwilling to accept the hand they had been dealt, trying to bend reality to a fixed notion of how the world ought to be. I had been a victim of that type of thinking myself. Much of what I'd pursued in my career and personal life was about trying to shape my world into how I thought things should be instead of accepting things as they were.

In drawing, I found an elegant teaching, grounded in seeing and doing rather than in thinking, about the beauty that can emerge first from becoming aware of what is real as opposed to what my mind imagines and then from accepting or surrendering to it. As I progressed in my art, I also attempted to interpret that information to create something expressive, something that was uniquely my own. Like a fingerprint, any bona fide drawing is unique to the draftsperson.

Even though I'd let go of thinking about business, I couldn't help but realize how these lessons could relate to it. Management was often about marshaling resources to shape the world to a vision of what the future could be. Yet often, being flexible enough to accept events and people, flaws and all, for what they actually were could be an invaluable skill, if not for the organization, at least for the manager. Because before you can move forward, you must know the reality of where you're standing—to accept what it was to be grounded, free of fantasy, free of magical or wishful thinking.

Drawing illuminated something else. Approaching a problem head on may be the most straightforward approach but not always the most creative or insightful. Complex business deals were like solving puzzles. Multiple stakeholders with interrelated and interacting sets of rights, obligations, needs, and wants often conspired to frustrate elegant solutions. Sorting it all out was creative in its own way, but oftentimes solutions were elusive. Without creative solutions, opportunity fails, profits compress, and deals die. Learning to see as an artist sees reminded me that figuratively turning things upside down—flipping a problem on its head—can convert a mindset fixed on how things should be to a mindset open to how things are. Sometimes, solutions hide in plain sight. In a way, our radical approach to Take-Two had illustrated this skill in action. I hoped our sabbatical did too.

At times, too, the problems themselves succumb to the limits of perception. Especially when viewed from the top of an organization, where detailed information can be hidden from sight, things can become distorted, and problems can remain invisible to the untrained eye.

I did not have a plan for how I would spend my days on sabbatical. But in drawing, I found a project that held endless fascination. The table at the center of our home became a dumping ground for large-format paper, pencils, erasers, and sharpeners. If I was trying to solve a drafting problem, like how to draw a portrait from a particular point of view, I went to the table to try my hand. When I ran into trouble, I jumped on YouTube to look for instructional videos on one or another aspect of drawing. If I needed a new tool or wanted to experiment with different media, I hopped on my motorbike and headed for the art supply store in an industrial district not far from the center of Ubud. Everywhere I went, I kept a small drawing pad and some pencils with me. They were my constant companions, and whenever I had downtime, I pulled them out. Even when I was not drawing, I saw differently, everywhere perceiving shape, form, shade, and edge.

My children ribbed me when they caught me squinting to better perceive changing light values like shadows or closing one eye to reduce my three-dimensional depth perception. I began to share with them the insights and showed them examples so they could see for themselves. "Can you see the way the nose throws a butterfly-shaped shadow on the face? Can you see how the sky on the horizon is a lighter blue than the sky overhead?" Sometimes they were interested, other times not. But I sensed they respected my curiosity and excitement about a new world opening up to me.

eleven

N ava was excited. She crouched in front of the computer, her hair still wet from her nighttime shower. She clicked on the Skype icon to open it and found the username for her classroom back in New York. Her teacher picked up on the third ring. She reminded the class where Nava was living and showed them where Indonesia was on the map. "Tell us what it's like, Nava."

"Good," Nava said, suddenly tongue-tied. She gave a few more monosyllabic answers, then her teacher turned to the class.

"Does anyone have any questions for Nava?" Silence. None of the kids knew how to communicate with Nava in this way. "I'm sure someone must have a question."

One brave child broke through the awkwardness. "What's the food like?"

Nava came to life. "Terrible! But there's this one place, Taco Casa, that has the best burritos in the world, and they deliver. And don't come here if you like pizza. It's much better in New York."

She took two more questions, and their short time was up. The whole episode lasted only fifteen minutes, but Nava lit up at the sight of familiar faces. By the time we got her to bed, I sensed her sadness return. "We can do that again if you like,"

Victoria said. Then she kissed Nava good night, pulled the mosquito netting around her bed, and turned off the lights.

ᔓ

The next day, an email arrived from Pak Andy, one of Sam's teachers. He called an urgent meeting of ninth- and tenth-grade parents to "address issues regarding weekend activities of some of our students."

That Wednesday, the parents and Andy gathered in the fourth-grade classroom as the sun set. Andy was about my age or perhaps a bit younger, and his hair was beginning to gray. That evening he wore his trademark batik shirt that fitted loosely around his slight build. Andy was a serious and committed educator who cared deeply about kids. I paid attention when he spoke.

Andy opened the meeting. "Some of our students have been reported in town drinking with some of the local kids. We've had problems with alcohol, especially homemade arrak, which often is laced with non-food-grade alcohol. Worse than that, we've heard reports of marijuana use."

He took on an ominous tone. "No kidding around, folks. You're not back in Europe, Australia, or the States. In this country, there's a death penalty for drug violations. The police don't need a search warrant. They can simply knock on the door, enter, and arrest your child. They've busted parties where only a single kid was smoking marijuana, but they arrested everyone in the house."

We'd thought there was no cause for concern for our own kids. We had good kids. Then again, how many parents were shocked when they found out their little angels were up to no good? Andy had planted the seed of doubt, and it scared me.

Our friend Luli offered a poignant perspective on the matter. She was a slight, energetic, thirtysomething British woman; a former editor of *Tatler* magazine in London; the wife of a local furniture entrepreneur; and the mother of three children, one of whom was attending Green School. In an alternate life, she could easily have been flashing credit cards in the shops on Kensington High Street. Instead, she followed her husband, Charles, to the far reaches of the developing world in search of exotic woods to convert into furniture and sell to major hotel chains. "Charles saved me from a boring London life." Asked for her favorite place in the world to live, Luli said, "I try to be present wherever I am."

Luli was also a deeply religious Christian. She and Victoria connected tightly. They both were committed to their respective religions, enjoyed the outdoors, and shared a passion for education. Driven at least partly by her religious beliefs, Luli often visited Bali's prison to offer friendship, support, and food to the inmates, particularly to the members of the Bali Nine, a group of Australians arrested for planning to smuggle heroin from Indonesia to Australia. Luli believed that at the time of their arrest, they were young and stupid and had made a terrible mistake. Now they were paying for it, potentially with their lives. They were on death row, appealing their sentences.

The prison was located in Kerobokan, a dilapidated area in the south, where rice fields had long ago been paved over. Unadorned, ominous, and wrapped in barbed wire, its walls had blocked the natural flow of traffic and forced vehicles to navigate around its massive girth. The rectangular structure now stood at the center of a traffic circle, a formidable reminder of the authority and power of the institution behind the building.

When Luli visited, she brought food and her young children with her, offering sustenance, companionship, and a semblance of family to these tragically anxious young men and one woman. She inserted herself into and was involved in their lives almost from the day they were arrested. She visited them weekly, cared for them, and prayed for them.

In a matter-of-fact manner, Luli described to us their life in prison, the hours she would spend in the sweltering, still air, first

in the waiting area outside and then in the tiny visitors' courtyard, where only a small patch of blue sky was visible.

The combination of Luli's stories of life inside Kerobokan
Prison and Pak Andy's meeting at Green School was enough to
put the fear of God in me. We had heard that if a kid was busted
for drugs by the police, there was an unspoken rule in Bali: the
family had twenty-four hours to pay a twenty-five-thousand-
dollar bribe, in cash, then pack their belongings and leave the
country. With every passing day, the fee went up by another
twenty-five thousand dollars. By the time a week had passed, the
file would have moved into the Indonesian police system and
out of the hands of the local cops.

I walked out of that meeting considering calling it quits. Sabbaticals were nice so far as they went, but I was unwilling to put
my family at this kind of risk. Victoria talked me down from
the ledge, assuring me that Sam, due to who he was and because
he was rarely on his own or away from our family, was not in
jeopardy.

That night I went to speak to Sam. "I know this isn't about
you," I said. "I know you don't do drugs, and I trust you. But I
need to remind you of what the pilot said on our flight from Singapore. The penalty in this country for drug violations is death.
So if you find yourself in a room with somebody doing any drugs
at all, you pick up and leave. Call me anytime, I'll come get you."

He looked at me blankly. "Just so you know, Daddy, I know
that marijuana, cocaine, and other drugs are illegal here, but it
just so happens that magic mushrooms are not. They blend them
into milkshakes, and I know exactly where they're sold, at a place
right in the center of town." I was shocked in the way parents
are shocked when they should not be, when teenagers behave
like teenagers. Sam's words reminded me that he was aging past
his innocent childhood. "But I don't do any of these things, and
I don't plan to. Don't worry about it."

I knew enough about teenagers to do the opposite when they
say, "Don't worry."

twelve שתים עשרה

I thought about what to pack for the bike trip to Java. The wet season in Bali had ended. The change was not abrupt, but I noticed fewer tropical downpours. Now quiet overcast skies gave way only to mild showers that lasted about an hour. I included some light raingear in my bag, just in case.

Before I set out, I sat next to Nava, who was reading on the couch, as she did most mornings before breakfast. "What was it I heard you saying to Oliver the other day about Green School?" I asked. I knew Oliver had asked her to tell him something she liked about Bali.

"No walls and no doors," she said. "Everything is open. Like being in the wilderness. I take a deep breath so I can have fresh air even inside the classroom."

I knew what she meant. Green School's buildings were veritable cathedrals made of bamboo, soaring from the jungle floor. Even the nails that held the wood together were bamboo. Three large, connected spiral structures, with round roofs thatched in local alang-alang grass, formed the center of the campus. The natural world that was core to the school's educational mission was literally all around and could be felt, seen, and heard.

I gave Nava a kiss on her forehead. "You know I'm going to Java for a few days, right?" She nodded, eager to get back to her book. "I'll see you when I get back, okay?" She pecked me on the cheek and returned to her reading.

〰

In the morning, I pedaled up to Green School, where John Hardy and the rest of the group waited in the parking lot. There were a dozen of us in all, mostly but not entirely Green School parents. Jon Ross made sure we didn't mill about for too long. We left on time at eight thirty to meet our guides in Bedugul, a mountain lake area in the center of the island about an hour away. John had arranged for our bikes to be transported ahead of us. Van support in Java would take our gear from one location to the next so that we wouldn't have to carry the extra weight on our bikes.

When we arrived in Bedugul, we quickly unloaded the bikes, filled our CamelBaks with water and our tires with air, and applied sunscreen. I knew it was time to go when Pak Andy's wife, Michelle, plugged in her earbuds and cranked up the music. Once jacked in, she would want to move her legs. Peter clipped a GoPro camera onto his helmet. "Movin' out!"

Jon took the lead. The route was a mountain road that started out easy. The main challenge was dodging opposing traffic that pulled into our lane to pass. About five kilometers in, we turned off the road onto a dirt track. The trail was so thick with underbrush that I often lost sight of the ochre earthen path. My tires crushed a thick carpet of dense flora as they rolled over.

A slight rain developed, and the single track became slippery with mud just as we hit a challenging segment. Off to one side, a deep ravine with no protective barrier opened to a valley floor below; on the other side was a mountain wall, thick with mud and brush roots. The soil in the mountain that day was so heavy with rainwater that it spouted spontaneously from the walled earth as if from a leaky bladder.

The path developed dips, some of them abrupt and deep. The only way to navigate the hollows was either to stop and walk the bike across or to use forward momentum and a little hop to jump over. Jon, one of the most experienced and skilled riders in our group, taught me that little maneuver. But as he turned a corner, he lost his balance. He instinctively unclipped his right foot from the pedal to touch the ground and set himself upright. But there was no footing. Instead of earth, there was only air. In a blink, he separated from his bike and sailed into the ravine below. He just disappeared.

Peter saw it happen and was stunned in disbelief. He dismounted and ran over to where Jon's bike lay. He called down below, "You all right? You okay, bud?" He picked up Jon's bike. There was no response to Peter's call.

Then a rustling crackled about fifty meters below. "I'm okay!" Jon clambered up the side of the ravine to the trail. Fortunately for him, a small tree had broken his fall. He suffered only minor scrapes. He maintained his British decorum. "I guess I caught a little bit of air there. Luckily, not too much." And then, "My heart is going kaboom." Following the advice given to anyone thrown from a horse, he got back in the saddle and carried on.

As we pressed forward, the path got even narrower. Up ahead, a river raged with fresh rainwater. The group stopped at its edge. The only way across was a makeshift bridge slapped together with bamboo slats that had rotted and become uneven with time. Michelle was nervous about going across, but there was no other way. She gritted her teeth and began to cycle, careful to look neither right nor left. The slats clattered as she rode over them. The loose frame of the bridge swayed. It took less than a minute to get across, but once there, she said, "I don't really want to do that again."

For me, these episodes were a reminder that there were so few protections and so many careless ways to fall ill or get injured in this part of the world—rabies from the dogs, dengue fever from mosquitos, car accidents from poorly designed roads. The list went on and on.

By afternoon, we rolled up sopping wet at the port of Gilimanuk, just in time to catch the ferry to Java, where support vans were waiting to take us to our hotel at the bottom of the Ijen volcano. By the time we arrived at the hotel, it was already getting dark. We grabbed our bags and a quick shower before settling in for dinner and a beer.

I sat next to Peter. We rehashed the day's adventures. Then he confided that he was up against a deadline. His sabbatical leave from the Canadian Broadcasting Corporation was coming to an end, and he had to decide whether to return to his job or call it quits and start something new. It was not an easy decision, but the conversation was common among expats living in Bali. Many thought about using a break as an off-ramp from one career path to the next. Peter and I batted around pros and cons. It was clear to me by the way he spoke that he wasn't going back to Canadian winters anytime soon.

I hadn't yet arrived at the crossroads of a decision like Peter's, but I knew it was coming.

Jon interrupted the dinner conversation. "Tomorrow's a big day, guys. We're going up Ijen. It's a tough ride, so get some sleep. We'll meet at the front of the hotel, bags packed, ready to hit the road at eight thirty."

I woke early the next morning and walked out my door onto the hotel's lawn. First light fell softly. Off in the distance, emerald-green rice terraces stepped slowly upward. Palm trees punctuated the wide landscape, and brief glints of sunlight flashed from the water in the distant irrigation canals. Beyond the rice fields, Mount Ijen rose majestically to tower over the entire scene. It sloped so evenly and beautifully into a symmetrical cone that it reminded me of the parabolic curve that Sam studied in high school math. The sense of beauty and wonder ceded to trepidation; I would be ascending to the top of the volcano that day.

I sat in a lawn chair for about twenty minutes and watched the light brighten, losing its early golden hue. Then I walked to the dining room and piled eggs and rice onto my plate. I ate hungrily in anticipation of the day's ride and then returned to my room to pack my bags.

Michelle was the first to be ready to leave. The others primped and milled about in the hotel's parking lot. Michelle filled her CamelBak with fresh water for the day and slung it over her back, then rode in tight circles waiting for everyone else to gather. It took a good twenty minutes to get our group together before John led us out in the direction of the massive volcano.

Michelle plugged in her earbuds. Music helped her get more power out of her legs. We passed through some villages and made our way up a slow incline. The initial riding was easy, but as the grade steepened, my breath shortened.

As we progressed up the slope of the dormant volcano, it dawned on me what a classically cone-shaped volcano would mean to a mountain biker. The slope would pitch ever steeper as it approached verticality. An hour into the ride, as we started to climb sharply, I downshifted to keep my cadence but quickly fell behind as Michelle pulled away. The ascent got even steeper, and I downshifted again. Soon, I lost sight of Michelle and was separated from everyone in my pack of riders. I pushed on, but it was slow going. As I continued to climb, the weather deteriorated. Fog settled in and blocked sunlight. I felt the mist on my face. The temperature dropped with the increased altitude. I could see my breath, something I hadn't experienced since the wintry day we left New York.

The road became even steeper and more broken. Asphalt gave way to a rough dirt road, which quickly dwindled to a bumpy path riddled with stones the size of footballs. The mist turned to steady rain. I pulled out the rain jacket I'd shoved into my CamelBak.

I continued to grind my way up the hill, painfully and slowly. I searched for another gear but there were none lower than the one I was in. I cursed my bike. I wanted the chain to move more smoothly through the gears, the wheels to grip the terrain, and the crank set to better translate the energy from my muscles to the drivetrain. The more I suffered, the more I wanted. But the bike wasn't responding to me. I cursed it again for not having more gears just as I cursed the trail for its relentlessly increasing pitch and for getting between the summit and me.

The road was now a broken path of boulders shouldered against one another. It was not really a road at all. I couldn't crank out another rotation, and my bike came to a stop. I tried to hop off quickly to catch my balance but couldn't unclip my shoes from my pedals fast enough and fell right over. Pain shot through my right shoulder as it hit a boulder. I picked up that damn bike and walked alongside it for a bit. Then to adjust for the slope, I pushed it from behind. I walked for about half a kilometer that way before I lifted the bike and balanced the frame on one shoulder. When I tired of that method, I hinged forward and lugged it on my back as if I were carrying a sack of stones.

One hour later, I reached a clearing. I had finally arrived at Paltuding Valley, an open area that served as the base station of a mining operation and featured a small *warung* offering coffee, snacks, and a little fire for warmth. All in all, the ride had taken five hours to climb just fourteen miles and a vertical ascent of eighteen hundred meters. John, nearly fifteen years my senior, had arrived a full thirty minutes ahead of me. He sat with the others, drinking coffee and waiting for the group to gather. I was utterly spent, exhausted by the punishing climb.

John pointed. "Look up. Behind you." Through breaks in the cloud cover, I could see that the valley was not the summit. The volcano's caldera was straight up, kilometers ahead. And there was no way to get there by bike. The only way was on foot, and the terrain was rocky and slippery.

Most of the group were there for the cycling and had little interest in hiking to the top, but Michelle and I did. Exhausted, hungry, and wet, we began to make the climb, leaving the rest of the group below.

Along the way, we passed young men, their cheeks a raging red, walking in single file down wet, slippery steps. Each carried two baskets connected by palm wood rods slung in balance over his shoulders. Each basket was filled with large yellow chunks of sulfur mined from vents in the surface of the mountain. The connecting rods strained and flexed as the men walked with a heavy, unstable gait. They looked tired, filthy, and hungry.

"I heard about these guys," Michelle said. "They get paid less than ten dollars a day to break their backs." She was a nurse married to a teacher. Was this a pointed remark aimed at the businessman? More likely the vestigial guilt of the college social-ist who, when he decided to go into business, wrote off such economic disparity as the way of the world.

We walked on. The rain grew heavy. A steady patter of water bounced off the hood of my jacket. I clambered to the top, grab-bing at rock outcroppings to lift and balance my body. It was cold, and my fingers stung from the freezing rain and abrasive rock. I couldn't understand how the miners managed to carry their loads over this terrain. Some wore flip-flops or rubber boots, but no one had ankle support. The slope was steep and unrelenting. The path became rocky, and the forest gave way to rock-strewn terrain. I felt my breath quicken.

"I'm only wearing flip-flops," Michelle said. "How the hell am I going to get down?" We forged ahead.

Finally, we reached the volcano's edge. Puffs of white steam swirled with yellow sulfur to create a sepia haze that rose from the surface. Low clouds formed a lid over the terrain. Rain whipped across the jagged, fractured lava rock and pelted my face like birdshot. Steep slopes walled in the crater lake. The remains of a dead tree gripped the mountainside, a life cut short by the poisoned environment. Below, decades of rainwater had accumulated to create a placid body of water more than six hun-dred feet deep that reflected brilliant robin-egg blue. Its stillness stood opposed to the violence of the volcanic eruption that cre-ated it. The accumulated water in the caldera of Mount Ijen in

Indonesia was the most acidic lake in the world, and the evaporating fumes were as toxic as the gas steaming through fissures in the rock beneath my feet.

Soaking wet, I shifted my toes and felt the mud squelch in my mountain-bike shoes. My damp clothes clung to my shivering skin. An acrid stench arose from below, the musty rotten-egg stink of sulfur mixed with oxygen, like someone had just lit a match. My eyes burned, and my throat was scratchy. I could almost feel the noxious air polluting my lungs. How could the miners inhale this stuff without any protection? I coughed as I fished inside my knapsack for a bandana to cover my nose and mouth. I came up empty. There was no protection against the toxicity.

It was as if I stood in a Hollywood set of a primordial offering ritual with fire, ash, and brimstone raining down. But there were no virgins to sacrifice at this volcano and no chanting. Instead of humans being tossed into the seething pit to appease imagined gods, a single line of miners filed in the opposite direction, out of the steaming crater, as if from the center of the earth.

Ijen had last erupted a dozen years earlier, a long while ago on the human scale but a mere blink in geological time. If an eruption were to occur again, as it almost certainly would, the poisoned water of the crater lake would pollute the irrigation systems below. The lake was a persistent environmental threat.

When meditators sit in mountain position or yogis stand in mountain pose, they evoke an image of dignity, strength, and immovability in the face of the elements. But that was not this mountain. Ijen was beautiful and powerful, yes, but it was also a hellscape made literally of fire and brimstone. The image of Ijen was the opposite of the Buddhist image of the ideal emotional mind: a storm raging on the ocean, where the tempest is at the surface, but below, in the ocean depths, calm reigns. At Ijen, the roar was hidden below.

I looked down again and felt a shiver of unreality. How had I arrived here? I'd walked away from a lucrative and exciting job as CEO of a public video game publisher that had released billion-dollar franchises. I had traveled around the world, first restructuring and then building an exciting and successful company. But something had been missing. I was leading a life not my own. I had felt unbalanced, and the partnership I was in wasn't feeding me. Success wasn't enough.

I turned to Michelle. "Ready?"

The muddy terrain was slippery and the decline steep. Michelle's wet feet slid forward and slammed into the thongs of her flip-flops with each step. Soon the thongs were cutting into the skin between her toes, and her pain worsened with every step.

I stepped in front of her. "Put your hands on my shoulders and lean on me." It helped break her forward momentum, which eased the pressure on the thongs. The clouds and the rain began to clear, and in the distance, we could see the summit of Mount Merapi, Indonesia's most active volcano, steaming like a simmering kettle.

When we arrived at the *warung*, the others were geared up and ready to go. We still had a lot of riding ahead of us, and it was getting late. We had to arrive at the hostel before dark. We mounted our bikes and set out.

As difficult as the broken road was to navigate on the way up, it was even more treacherous on the way down. My forearms and fingers were cramping from the grip. My knuckles were white. Peter stopped to take some video footage and called out to give me some downhill riding tips: lighten up on the grip, and trust the bike and its shock absorbers to do the work. I didn't quite close my eyes, like Luke Skywalker placing absolute trust in the Force, but I did ease my grip on the handlebars, bend my knees slightly to settle into a crouch position, unclench my teeth, and relax my shoulders.

All of a sudden, the topography loosened up for me. Instead of fighting it, I let it carry me. I didn't navigate around rocks or slam into them; I bounced over them. I didn't squeeze my brakes on steep declines; I let the bike rip. It seemed as if there was nothing between me and the ground below. The bike was a mere extension of my body. Once or twice, on a rough incline, I stopped in my tracks; this time I stayed upright with my shoes clipped into the pedals, pulled on the handlebars, and hopped from one rock to the next. The ride became fluid and graceful. As in any relationship, once I learned to trust, my bike delivered, and I became stronger. I felt I'd broken through some barrier and left something behind. It was a soaring emotion.

I dismounted my bike to take in the moment and mopped my face with a sleeve. I smelled the fragrant soil. I wondered at the moss-covered stones, the giant roots of hardwood trees, and the luscious leaves of primary rainforest around me. In the distance, a powerful waterfall crashed.

The remainder of the descent from the volcano was a dirty, wet mess but a lot of fun. Muck from my bike spattered across my clothes and caked my face. I hollered joyfully as my bike screamed through murky puddles. By the time we arrived at the hostel Catimor Homestay, the sun was setting and my face was a fractal of mud.

Catimor wasn't much to speak of. The rooms were musty but dry, the showers had hot water, and the evening meal made up in warmth what it lacked in taste. Some of the others in our group stayed up after dinner to reminisce about the day's ride in the hostel's aging Jacuzzi. I went to my room and, fully clothed, collapsed on my bed and closed my eyes. I slept deeper than I had in years.

Ꮑ

The next morning, we had a relatively short, easy rolling ride to Bondowoso at the other end of Ijen National Park. The ride was about fifty kilometers, mainly downhill, with about twenty kilometers of moderately broken road that was easy to navigate. We passed cocoa bean plantations and again saw workers breaking their backs, this time to pick beans. We passed Blawan, one of four government-owned coffee plantations that took advantage of the volcanic soil, elevation, and rain to produce some of

Java's best coffee. The women who picked the berries in the field were covered from head to toe to protect themselves from the sun, which, when it beat down, was brutal.

We stopped to taste some of the local coffee. The *warung* served up a batch from beans that had been freshly roasted, but the coffee tasted bitter to me and left a coarse feeling in my mouth as it went down. A black sludge of coffee grounds lingered at the bottom of the cup. I wondered what Asher would have thought.

I had a growing awareness of how our group must have looked to the locals: a bunch of Westerners in colorful outdoor gear, fancy bikes, and helmet cams. I thought about the juxtaposition of our presence against the miners who toiled in a toxic environment or the farm workers who slaved in the searing heat. Here, on this trip through southeastern Java, I saw true suffering wrought of the need for the basic necessities of life.

I thought of *metta* meditation, which cultivates compassion by imagining sending kindness to others with each exhale and receiving their suffering with each inhale. Compassion was a core Buddhist ethic that began with compassion for the self and ended with compassion for all sentient beings. I closed my eyes, took in a deep breath as I thought about those workers, and exhaled slowly. It was a strange response for me, someone who would ordinarily think about concrete ways to help or otherwise take action. There was little I really could do. Yet I recognized the benefit of cultivating compassion in my own mind in the face of their suffering and the harm to me if I were to be as indifferent as a mountain to their suffering. I also tried to instill compassion in my children, some of whose friends—and ours—seemed to take for granted their windfall into privilege.

I took in another deep breath. Then another. And another.

At Bondowoso the vans picked us up to take us to the city of Malang, a five-hour drive made even longer by Javanese traffic. The group had arranged to stay at a city hotel, but I had other plans. A local internet entrepreneur, Steve Christian, had invited me to stay with him in his guesthouse.

Steve was ethnically Chinese, a group considered outsiders
in Indonesia and, because of their economic success, discrimi-
nated against. It was a narrative familiar to someone like me,
whose Jewish grandparents lived in Eastern Europe before and
after the Second World War. Steve, having sold more than one
business to US internet companies, was successful, especially
by Indonesian standards. Yet he shared the insecurity of many
ethnic Chinese Indonesians. He lived in a large home behind
an alarmed, wrought-iron gate. Like early American immigrants
who changed their names in order to better fit in, Steve's name
connoted nothing at all Chinese.

With Indonesia's economy growing at a rate twice that of the
United States, and with smartphones only beginning to pen-
etrate, I was keenly interested in what Steve was up to. I yearned
for a business discussion. I couldn't help but sniff the scent of
new opportunities. But it seemed more like a pleasurable game
than a serious endeavor or compulsion.

Steve and I ate Chinese takeout and talked about business
and the ventures he was nurturing. I felt an easy affinity toward
him, and our business conversation was neither fraught nor
complicated.

In the morning, Steve drove me to the hotel where my group
was staying. I joined them for a ride up another volcano, Mount
Bromo, on the outskirts of the city. Its caldera had erupted only
six months earlier and was still active with tremors and periodic
ash eruptions. Once a year, the people of East Java traveled up
Mount Bromo to make offerings of fruit and vegetables and, to
appease ancient deities, to sacrifice livestock by throwing them
into the caldera. Believing it would bring them good luck, some
locals tempted fate and made the dangerous trek into the caldera
to retrieve the sacrifices.

Having had my fill of toxic calderas as well as personal sacrifices, I had no intention of making it to the top. We stayed at
lower elevations, but the riding was still steep and difficult. At
times, I needed to lift my bike onto my shoulders to get past

difficult terrain. My body was spattered with dirt and blood from the various scrapes I took. Steep ravines were always present, always a danger, but I was more confident in the saddle. I let instinct and muscle take over. I tried not to think of the volcanic rumble that growled only a few kilometers away.

By the time we returned to Malang, my legs hurt badly. I darted through traffic to the drop-off point from which John had arranged for our bikes to be transported back to Bali. From there, we piled into cars destined for the Surabaya airport and a flight home.

On the small Air Asia plane, I thought about our ride. I was beaten to the top of the mountain by a man nearly fifteen years older than me and had to carry my bike to make it at all. At another time in my life, that would have bruised my ego, even if I knew it was silly. This time, I felt no shame. Getting to the top was the main thing, as was experiencing the grinding effort it required.

I pictured Ijen, its power and beauty but also its toxicity. I remembered what it had been like for me in New York, when I tried to find another gear but could not, when I reached the top of an organization only to discover the view was not what I'd imagined. I would need to find another way to exist, to be in this world, not with the explosive energy of an Ijen, but with the power, dignity, and sanctity of a different kind of mountain.

Landing at the local terminal in Bali, with no customs or immigration to clear, I felt for the first time like a native and that I belonged. I had returned home, and it felt good.

thirteen ׀ שלש

I returned to our villa from the airport that Friday afternoon. Shoes of all sizes lined the entrance to the front door, a sure sign that the family was in. Putu's mother was cooking a vegetarian Indonesian meal, and the smell of frying shallots, like teenage body odor, wafted from the kitchen. Even though Nava had once proclaimed, "I'd rather starve!" eventually she tried new Indonesian flavors and discovered her capacity to adapt to and even be curious about new foods. Her favorite: *tempeh manis*, freshly made tempeh cut into small pieces, fried until crispy, tossed in a sweet sauce, and sautéed again with chili peppers and garlic. On the menu this time was *cap cay*, a Chinese-style vegetable stir-fry with plenty of cabbage.

Friday nights were special in our family. We regularly celebrated the Jewish Shabbat with a large meal. Well before an internet Sabbath became fashionable in some technology circles, our family unplugged all our electronics for twenty-four hours each week. There were no computers, no phones, and no television. Instead of the pseudohuman contact of electronic media, we made eye contact with each other. We played board games, lingered over meals, and lazed around. But as the day drew to a close, the kids typically got fidgety, and the moment it was over, the screens flashed open faster than an Intel processor.

Early in my career and marriage, I'd made a commitment never to miss Friday-night dinner at home. Even when work required that I travel regularly from New York to Asia, my commitment to my family to be home Friday night was firm. One Friday, I traveled back from Tokyo to New York, survived on cat-naps for forty-eight hours, then turned right around and headed back to Japan. It hadn't always been easy for me, but after many years of struggle, I learned to appreciate more fully the magic of the day and what it meant for our family to be still.

Now in Ubud, we adopted a new custom to our Friday-night ritual. We all wore semiformal dress, Bali-style: sarongs and sashes. The boys, including me, were at first uncomfortable wearing what Oliver called skirts. But it was completely normal in Bali, and over time it became normal in our family.

When I returned from Java that Friday, we waited until dark to eat. Putu and her mother had left the food on the outdoor table, the plates covered in mesh domes to protect the food from bugs. Just as we prepared to begin our meal, Nava did or said something that set Rita off. Rita and Nava regularly argued about the real estate of the bed they shared, each accusing the other of violating her sovereign territory. This was different. Something had happened. I did not see or hear what it was, but before I knew it, they flew at each other, each screaming at the other that she was "the worst sister ever."

With the ear-splitting conflict, Sam grew silent. His face took on a my-family-is-completely-nuts expression.

Oliver got into the mix. "Rita, calm down!"

I shot back, "Oliver, you're not the parent around here."

"Yeah, whatever." Oliver and Sam beat a retreat to their room and now were separated from the family.

I looked wide eyed at Victoria. She threw down her napkin. "You take care of it. I've been dealing with it all week." And I'd been away, just as I often had been in New York.

I talked to Rita when she settled down about an hour later. I realized that Oliver was involved too, which didn't surprise me.

Theirs had always been a charged relationship. While Rita had made good friends at Green School and generally was in good spirits, her relationship with Oliver still had moments of desperate conflict. Oliver had hurled an insult at her that hit home. Now Rita slid backward. Although angry with Oliver, she lashed out all around.

Or maybe it had something to do with my being gone for the week.

Victoria and I finally herded everyone to the table. The food was cold, and we mostly ate in silence.

〰

The next morning, bright light pierced the curtains and spilled a golden puddle on our stone floor. A slice of moon lingered beyond the rice fields, and an errant cloud wisped in the air currents. At breakfast, the conversation was jovial. Something about family life had become more resilient; tensions eased quicker, and that morning felt like a new beginning. The kids asked about my trip to Java, and I heard about what was happening in school. We worked on the jigsaw puzzle and played Boggle.

While the kids settled into a game of Settlers of Catan, Victoria and I talked about Pak Chris's Sea to Summit field trip. In what once might have been a tense conversation in which each of us wanted to make sure the other had heard our concerns, we instead quickly found common ground and decided to let Oliver go. He would need a little encouragement, but courage was something that seemed to come easily to Oliver. In the afternoon, friends dropped by to splash around in the pool and graze on the apple pie and brownies that we picked up on Fridays at Bali Buda, just off Ubud's main road.

〰

The next day, I sat with my drawing pad on my lap, pencil in hand, contemplating a flowering plant in our backyard. Victoria said, "Are you going all Gauguin on us?" I rolled my eyes, and she laughed. Among the myriad ways I was unlike Gauguin, I had no idea how to draw the human figure, let alone paint it. Still, Gauguin also discovered art in his middle age. He taught himself just as I was doing. And Victoria did give me the idea to focus on Gauguin-like subjects. After all, I was living in Bali, he in Tahiti. For an American, the similarities were close enough, and for a moment, I allowed the comparison. Gauguin stayed in Tahiti for two years before returning to France and ultimately resided in the South Pacific permanently. I downloaded a copy of W. Somerset Maugham's *The Moon and Sixpence*, a fictionalized version of Gauguin's life. As I read, I fantasized about what it would be like to accept the call to be an artist rather than a businessman, extend my sabbatical in Bali, and draw Balinese models. I wanted to dismiss the thought, but it reasserted itself in my mind, so I let it loiter a few moments longer than I should have.

I searched the internet for art classes in the area. Mostly what I came across related to art therapy, yet another portal to Ubud's healing culture. But one class, life drawing, caught my eye. It was being offered at the back of an art gallery on Ubud's main road, Jalan Raya, not far from my home.

One afternoon, I stopped by Pranoto's Art Gallery. It was right next door to Body and Soul, where a sixty-minute massage cost one hundred thousand rupiah, or about ten dollars. Pranoto greeted me as walked in. Already in his fifties, he was a slender Balinese painter. His graying beard was stained from too many cigarettes, his teeth from too much coffee. He cut a figure taller than most local men and spoke, in perfect English, with a purpose. As we talked, I sensed his deep commitment to his art and Ubud's artist community.

He didn't so much teach a class as hold drawing sessions for a group of local artists. I told him I wanted to attend. "*Tidak apa apa*," he said. "No problem. Come back Wednesday morning at ten o'clock. Bring your own materials." The cost was twenty thousand Indonesian rupiah, about two dollars.

That Wednesday, I arrived fifteen minutes early. Artists trickled in carrying canvases, large-format paper pads, easels, and boxes filled with paint and charcoal. I had a single number-two pencil, an eraser, a sharpener, and a pocket sketchbook.

A draped chaise longue occupied the center of the room. A single bright lamp hung overhead, and a pot of coffee brewed in the rear of the studio. The other artists seemed to know each other well and engaged in casual conversation. Pranoto recognized me and motioned me to sit. "Anywhere on the floor you'd like. Make sure you get a good view of the model. Cushions are in the back." I sat cross-legged and waited.

At ten o'clock, a pretty Balinese model entered the room. She wore a batik sarong, the traditional fabric of Indonesia, tied above her chest. I wondered for a moment why she looked familiar but soon recognized her. She was a waitress at the Bali Buda café, just down the street, where I often drank tea and read the papers. As she approached the chaise longue, the room fell silent. She sat, removed her sarong, and retied it around her waist. My heart quickened at the sight of her naked torso. I knew life drawing meant nudity, but I wasn't quite prepared for it.

The model struck a pose and looked at Pranoto for approval. He coached her, asking her to move an arm or to shift her body to the side. Then he bellowed, "Two-minute pose!" Pranoto came over to me. "These short poses are just a warm-up. Throw away your early drawings. Longer poses come later."

I recognized Pranoto's quick drawing exercises. They were meant to encourage Edwards's shift from L-Mode to R-Mode. Accessing the right side of the brain could not be switched on like a light. It wasn't like moving from one task to another. R-Mode needed to be seduced to center stage, to be teased and warmed up. Short drawing exercises, like short poses, were one of the tricks of the trade. Even experienced artists needed to get their heads in the right place before getting down to business.

The silence of the room gave way to a cacophony of scratches. The scraping sounds of charcoal, pencils, pens, and brushes all merged into something less than a symphony. Artists nodded like bobbleheads as they shifted their gazes from the model to their work and back again. I turned my attention to my own work. I felt the tension of staring keenly at a seminude model and could not quite settle down. I fell back on what I had learned so far about art and tried to focus on shapes, lines, and angles. Soon the nudity fell out of my consciousness and was replaced by the business of capturing the human figure in two-dimensional space. Through a series of poses that increased in length up to twenty minutes, I struggled to faithfully reproduce in hard graphite the image of the model in front of me.

I concentrated on breaking down into components what I was observing. I slowly deconstructed the image of the model in order to understand how I was handling it in my mind. I focused on the shapes of the shadows as they fell across the model's face and body. I stared at her for long minutes at a time, slowing down my thought processes so that I could take in hidden information.

It made me understand not only how my mind quickly processed information but also how, in drawings, the slightest mark that hinted at a familiar image would cause the viewer's brain to quickly fill in information to create the full image in their own minds. A slight vertical mark below a set of eyes would immediately be understood as a nose even though the line on its own bore little resemblance to a nose.

Seeing the way an artist sees, for me, required me to create space and slow down the speed with which my mind constructed the image. It demanded intense focus. I became so lost in what I was doing that the chatter in my mind was silenced. When Edwards's L-Mode/R-Mode shift kicked in, the words of my inner voice disappeared. In their place, I could see only what was in front of me and on my page. I was in the here and now rather than some time or place in the future or the past. I fell into it as if into a trance.

In the 1990s, University of Chicago's Mihaly Csikszentmih-alyi introduced a concept that he called "flow." Flow was focused attention at its peak. It's what happens to artists when they get lost in their work, when they are so focused that everything else, every thought unrelated to the task at hand, falls away.

When I was in the video game business, flow had been used to describe the deep involvement of players in some games. But I didn't experience it there because I was multitasking and dis-tracted by any number of emails, meetings, and calls that demanded my attention. But now, simple pencil and paper drew me in. I was focused on the effort, not the result. I had no expectations of myself. What drove me was pure interest, pure curiosity, and pure amazement at what I could perceive simply by being aware and engaged.

Pranoto called a five-minute break. I wandered the room to see what other artists were doing and what I could learn. I asked questions. Here and there I coaxed a drawing tip. Even though we were all drawing or painting the same model, no two styles or techniques were the same. The interpretations of that model were wildly different from one artist to the next. They reaffirmed the idea that expression is unique to each individual and that raw information, in art and elsewhere, is much less interesting than the interpretation and insights derived from it.

About halfway through the three-hour session, Pranoto called a long break. I stopped to talk to Leo, an American who I guessed was in his seventies. Leo was a retired philosophy profes-sor who had taught in Edinburgh. He drew in a style that used many short marks as opposed to longer edge lines. He brought his own stool on which to sit, a collapsible aluminum easel, and a tube into which he rolled his drawing paper.

I asked Leo to show me his work. He pulled out a portfolio. Most of his drawings had a sepia background and were smaller than the large-format paper I had seen him use. I asked him how he got that effect.

"I draw in graphite," he told me, "then I scan my work into Photoshop and play with it."

I asked what he did with all his finished work.

"Give them as gifts. If I get invited to dinner, I'll bring a small drawing instead of wine. My hosts seem to like it."

When the break ended, I went back to my cushion and began again. The poses went on until, at one o'clock, Pranoto called, "Time!"

The hours had zipped by like minutes. I felt no distraction, no need for coffee or a snack. I had been utterly lost in intense concentration. Each stroke of my pencil seemed like the only thing that mattered in the universe. My sense of self—my ego—completely surrendered to the sense of presence in the immediate moment.

The model stretched her limbs, which must have ached from being perfectly still for as long as twenty minutes at a time, often in challenging poses. I packed up my things and waited for Victoria to pick me up on our motorcycle.

When she arrived, my fingertips were black with graphite, hers black with mud from mountain biking with Michelle that morning. I complained about the quality of my work and how difficult it was.

Victoria sat behind me on our motorbike, her arms wrapped around my waist, as we motored toward Sari Organics, a restaurant and farm set in the middle of a rice field. We parked the bike by the road and walked a few hundred yards down a path through rice paddies, where maturing stems swayed in the moist breeze. When we arrived, I ordered a green papaya salad. Victoria ordered vegetarian *nasi campur*. I told her how I'd felt free of distractions, in a zone so private, so clear, and so deep in focused concentration that there was nothing else in the world to think about but the next mark on the page. I was exhilarated.

Until I pulled out my drawings. In my best drawing, I had shown the model at least twenty pounds heavier than she was. Her hands looked like claws, and her lower body was compacted to the point that her legs looked like they belonged to Sponge-Bob SquarePants. There was no balance in the composition. There was no sense of composition at all.

But Victoria was complimentary and encouraging. "It's just a start," she said. "Keep at it. You'll improve. This whole thing is really cool."

She said nothing about the nudity.

fourteen ཡེཊ

The next Sunday, I woke early, ahead of Victoria and the kids, and stepped out onto the back patio, glassy with the fresh rainwater of a dawn shower. The air was redolent with the fragrance of newly moist soil, and the sun was just beginning to break through the clouds. I saw Made removing gecko droppings from the floor of the villa as part of his morning routine. He smiled broadly to wish me good morning. "*Selamat pagi*, Mister Ben."

"*Selamat pagi*, Made."

I walked to the gazebo to prepare for a yoga session while everyone slept. I looked at my smartphone to download a podcast and scrolled past David Farmar, an instructor who taught a particularly aggressive style of yoga known as Baptiste. He was my standard podcast when I could not make it to Yoga Barn. I chose instead an instructor new to me, Nikki Wong, a yogi from Northern California who recorded her classes and posted them online.

I unrolled my mat onto the gazebo's teak floorboards, careful to avoid a patch of sunshine that escaped the roof's shade. Practicing yoga under the sun's blazing heat would be unbearable. I removed my shirt and stood barefoot, wearing only a pair of shorts. I felt the cool tropical breeze against my body and popped in my earbuds.

I stood at the top of my mat and listened to Nikki's instructions to set an intention. When yoga teachers instructed me to set an intention, I had once struggled with the concept. I had no idea what they had meant. But now I understood. Intention was doing something deliberately so that it has meaning. Intention was what was missing in Malcolm Gladwell's well-known ten-thousand-hour rule that many hours of practice were required to achieve excellence. It was the intention to improve while putting in those hours that was crucially important. Just showing up didn't do it.

I had attended many business meetings where the chair of the meeting asks each individual around the table, "Are you present?" or "Are you in?" Like setting an intention, it was a way of establishing presence. As a manager and a leader, it was easy for me to distinguish who was present and who wasn't, who wanted to be in the room and who didn't. Some had the patience and the commitment to participate, while others consistently peeked at their smartphones or arrived late and left early. I too had been in situations where I was not present, where I was performing a task in which I had no interest. There was neither joy nor value in those tasks. Without presence or intention, the people around the boardroom table might as well be telling each other jokes.

I checked in and listened to Nikki ask me to form mountain pose: stand straight, big toes touching, inner thighs turned slightly inward, and hands in a prayer position at the chest. I imagined a straight vertical plumb line that ran from the crown of my head to the bottom of my heels to form the pose. I felt the full force of my feet touching the mat and focused on that tactile sensation. Much as in meditation, mountain position in yoga evoked in me strength, weight, and quiet force.

I directed my attention to my breathing. I placed my hands at the front of the mat, feet at the back, and hips scooped up into the air to form the most basic of poses, downward-facing dog. I breathed slowly and carefully, creating an ocean sound by narrowing my throat passage as I inhaled slowly. The air filled my lower belly, my lower ribcage, and then my upper chest.

Nikki talked me through some warm-up poses and then picked up the pace. I flowed from one pose to the next. High push-up, low push-up. Up-dog, down-dog. Inhale, exhale. I hopped to the front of my mat and then flew to the back of it and squeezed. Heat built up and sweat began to form. I brought my attention back to my ocean breath, making it loud and witnessing it as if it were not my own, as if my sense of ego were slowly being exhaled from my body. I felt both engaged and detached, simultaneously inside and outside of my own head.

I looked down. The bright patch of yellow sunlight arched toward me. I reached back into a peaceful warrior pose, then forward to a triangle pose. I witnessed my breath again in detached observation, watching my poses unfold just as I watched my thoughts in meditation.

I began to wonder about the transitions between the poses. Like the poses themselves, transitions require integrity, grace, and dignity. Exiting one posture and charging on to the next without attention and focus risked collapsing the whole situation into a jumbled mess.

Yoga transitions were a metaphor for other areas of my life. Sabbatical was a personal and professional change for me, but I could recognize that it was only a temporary condition, perhaps only a transition. It was easy to mistake it for something more permanent, but the lesson from yoga was clear: stay too long in transitions and the sense of grounding vanishes; hurry through transitions and the opportunity to set up a strong next position is lost.

Victoria and I had met expats in Bali who had confused temporary change with enduring situations. They stayed in Bali too long and began to lose touch with Western society. Some had found genuine belonging in Bali, but others seemed to be in a state of eternal transition, never quite finding their footing in either Bali or their home territories. I tried to convince myself that I needed to use Bali as a stepping-stone to the next phase of my professional and personal life. But the notion of staying longer nagged at me.

Impossibly, Nikki called through my earbuds, "Where did you go? Where did you go?" It was as if she had entered my mind. "Bring your attention back to your breath. Check in. Where did you go?"

Sweat practically squirted from my forehead. That bright spot of sunshine was nearly at my mat. I was tired but felt my breath and shifted into relaxation. I wrapped my torso around for a twisted lunge. I relaxed into the pose and held it, with each exhale wringing my body like a wet towel. I grimaced with the effort and then lost my balance. My back leg failed, and my knee fell to the mat. I recovered quickly and reassumed the pose and held it until it was time for the next.

In tree pose, I gazed intensely at a point in space—a knot in the hardwood frame of the gazebo—to enhance my balance. I stared, trying to hold my balance standing on one leg, back arched, and arms reaching skyward. My focus strayed, and my balance went with it. I fell to the side as my body followed my mind.

In yoga, balance derives from the proper placement of limbs, head, and torso in relation to each other. In art, balance suggests itself when color, shape, and line are composed in a way that defines a work. In business, balance requires all elements of an enterprise to dovetail to create a competitive edge. It isn't enough to get costs aligned with revenue to create profit. Without having a point in the distance to focus on, balance, strength, and purpose become difficult, and the business is thrown off-kilter and falters. In yoga as elsewhere, to lose attention is to risk collapse.

Again, I heard Nikki: "Where did you go? Where did you go?"

I brought my attention back to the gazebo and settled down on my belly, reaching back to grab my feet. By extending my legs while simultaneously resisting them with my arms, I lifted my chest and arched my back to create the shape of a bow. In the next pose, I lay my right shin across the front of the mat, left leg extended behind me, thigh pressed against the mat, then folded torso over shin and dropped into half-pigeon pose.

What else can you drop? What else can you let go of?

The anguish I'd felt over leaving a life in the pursuit of excellence had melted away over the previous months. In its place, I felt joy again. I judged less and smiled more. I became interested in other people. I felt closer to my children and, especially, my wife. We spent all our free time together. Not every couple could survive that kind of closeness after nearly twenty years of being together, but for us it was joyful.

Where did you go?

I lifted my body from pigeon pose. The tension in my hip and lower back released over the course of ten breaths. I flowed through several more seated poses until I finally arrived at corpse pose, lying on my back perfectly still and feeling the supportive grounding of the floor against my body. After more than an hour of movement, of doing, corpse was a few moments of simply being.

Bright sunlight had already invaded my mat, but I would not get out of its way. Instead, I surrendered to it and felt it heat my skin. A few moments later, I sat at the top of the mat with my legs crossed in front. I felt grounded, centered, and unflappable. I placed my hands in a prayer position with my thumbs between my eyes and bowed my head, expressing gratitude for nothing and to nobody in particular.

fifteen ｜ ᜀᜇ

S am returned home from school, dropped his books in a
chair, and paced, frowning and muttering, from one end
of the house to the other. His class had watched *Tapped*,
a film about the environmental and health hazards of plastic-
bottled water. It was a heavy-handed video with a strong point
of view, but it raised his awareness that even something as simple
and ubiquitous as bottled water could have multifaceted rami-
fications. I was surprised that Sam was so affected. I had never
before heard him express an opinion about anything that didn't
impact him directly.

"It makes me kind of mad." He removed his laptop from his
backpack and showed me an image of the great garbage patch, a
huge collection of debris floating in the Pacific Ocean. It was
a vortex of the world's plastic trash swept together by the ocean's
circular currents. And it was enormous. I flashed for a moment
to the miniature gravitational water vortex that was supposed to
power Green School but never quite worked properly. Some
things at Green School were simply aspirational.

"There's one in the Atlantic too," he said. Without my prodding, he volunteered some action. "Can we stop using plastic
water bottles?" We discussed it at dinner that night, and the
family agreed to stop drinking from plastic bottles and instead

carry small canteens. We also vowed to stop using the plastic bags that came with every trip to the grocery store and littered the water around Bali's beaches.

A few weeks later, on Earth Day, Sam requested we turn out the lights for one hour at night. We sat in the dark and ribbed Sam about his "hour of power." But I was taken by Sam's own emerging power. I sensed in him a dawning awareness of issues larger than those in front of his nose.

It wasn't only a political awakening that I noticed. Sam's and his siblings' creativity emerged too. Sam and some of the kids in his class formed a band, with him on electric guitar. A few weeks later, on spring vacation, we took a side trip to Rajasthan, India, where Sam and Oliver shot a music video of a song that Oliver's music class had written about water conservation. With edgy camera angles and staccato shots of Oliver rapping amid a variety of settings—markets, temples, dunes, hills, and the Taj Mahal—among locals, elephants, camels, and his family, Oliver performed "The Water Rap," exhorting listeners, in a catchy and humorous way, to conserve water and poking fun at Green School's self-composting toilets. Back home, Sam and Oliver edited the video and released it on the internet under the label Sabbatical Records.

I asked Sam if he thought his time at Green School was changing him. "It's cool to be in an international school and get to know kids from all over the place." Back home, his social milieu was uniform. His friends shared more or less similar backgrounds, the school curriculum was circumscribed, and the balance of learning tipped in favor of tradition and convention over exploration and creativity. Green School felt expansive to him. Sabbatical was apparently a gift not only to Victoria and me, with the kids along just for the ride.

〰

Victoria's phone calls, which had been tapering off, were staging a comeback. Victoria had helped her organization find a space before she left, and they had put money into designing its build-out, but now the owner was backing out. Victoria felt responsible and wanted to help deal with it. She wasn't able to handle this crisis in absentia, and she took it hard. "I can't even succeed at what they need me to do."

ᨣ

Asher and Peter invited me on another of their afternoon bike rides. By then, I had learned how to handle myself better on Indonesian terrain. We started, as usual, at Green School, worked our way through the commercial traffic of Mambal, then took a jeep track behind a large field. We rode through bush and rice paddies on a single track that emptied onto a paved road. To my left, a large field hosted a makeshift billboard: "This Land Is Not for Sale." I had thought about buying a small place in Bali to own a bit of paradise. Besides, it was probably a good investment. My commercial logic was that Asia generally was riding the coattails of India's and China's hypergrowth. The raft of newly minted millionaires and billionaires being created would want their slice of heaven too. And there was only one Bali. But while the call of commerce returned to me, buying real estate in Bali was a complicated affair. Families sometimes sold their compounds for a fast profit only to spend the money quickly, often with disastrous results to family and society. That sign was a voice of protest and I needed to listen. I fought my instincts, let compassion overrule economic reason, and noted the change in my attitude.

With some hairy turns and short, steep climbs, we pulled into Ubud to end the afternoon ride. I followed Asher and Peter, this time on my bike, as they bounced down some stairs. I had all the confidence of an experienced mountain biker. An art gallery about one hundred yards away caught my eye. I made a note to return when I wasn't covered in sweat and mud.

One week later, Victoria and I visited and met the artist, I Wayan Karja. He was my age, spoke a soft English, and was happy to share his story. Karja had studied in the United States and had exhibited broadly outside Indonesia. I found him unusual because he was one of the few painters I had met who could verbalize his artistic intention. His paintings were abstract and minimalist. Some were color fields; others created circular movements that he said were like a mandala, a Hindu symbolic representation of the world. But his interpretation was the opposite of symbols. Instead of the figurative and iconic details of traditional mandalas, he tried to distill his to pure abstraction, to convey only the energy and movement of the mandala.

Karja led us through his studio. Racks of completed canvases stood next to his work area. Tubes of paint were neatly arrayed on a worktable. His work area, like his paintings, was clean and neat. A giant canvas lying flat on the floor was being prepared for his next piece. He led us to the gallery, flooded with natural tropical light, that I'd seen from my bike.

Victoria and I walked around and considered his paintings. We were taken by two of them especially. One he called *Meditation*, a work in dynamic blues with a subtle billowing shape in the center that he said was his interpretation of breath. We were concerned that it was too large for our home in New York. The other was a warm color field of reds and orange. In this painting, like many of his others, Karja painted a dark cleft in the middle of the right-hand edge to convey a Balinese sense of balance, a unity of opposing forces. Over the course of a few days, we agreed on a price, and the painting was ours.

I was taken by Karja's work. To a non-Balinese, it was accessible. It touched on two core practices that I was developing: meditation and art. And it spoke to some of the themes I'd been struggling with: the sense of balance in my life and the quest for a feeling of grounding and centeredness, even as I knew I had more work to do on that front—on all those fronts.

sixteen ᝉᝍᝄ

I t was late spring back in New York when Victoria and Oliver returned there to attend a family affair. Before they left, Victoria and I had searched for something special for the rest of us to do while they were gone. We settled on a side trip to Sumatra to visit Gunung Leuser National Park, one of two remaining habitats of the Sumatran orangutan. To the north of the island was the region of Aceh, the closest land point to the epicenter of the 2004 Indian Ocean earthquake. The resulting tsunami had destroyed the region.

We flew to Medan and from there took a taxi to the tiny village of Bukit Lawang. I kept a curious eye out the window as we escaped the traffic and motorcycle exhaust of the city. The urban sprawl soon gave way to countryside. As we drove along, we saw that wide swaths of rainforest had been clear-cut. Gone were the foliage and hardwoods. In their place, rows upon rows for miles upon miles of palm trees—periodically interspersed by a palm-oil processing plant—lined the landscape. The soil was a muddy rust-colored muck, devoid of green cover. Truck tracks rutted the dirt roads. Discarded palm fronds littered the roadside. These were no quaint farms but large industrial complexes that visibly injured the earth.

The ride took longer than expected, but by late afternoon, the taxi arrived at Gotong Royong, a village just a ten-minute walk from Bukit Lawang, which was inaccessible by car. A slight young man from the bungalow we'd rented met us to help with our bags. We walked up a single track, he in his flip-flops, we in our American hiking boots. The bungalow had two levels, the lower of which lay down steep stairs and rested near the banks of the swirling, fast-moving Bohorok River, which flowed between the bungalow and the national park.

We dropped our bags and prepared to settle in. I called to my kids, "Boys on the top level, girls below."

The young porter pulled me aside. "Mister, the little girls should stay on the top level." He explained that a few years earlier, a flash flood came crashing down from the hills above and wiped out everything in its path, including the village and more than two hundred people. "Just in case."

"Wait. What?"

I had been in Indonesia long enough to know that bad things could happen easily and often. The fear response in my brain lit up, beginning in the amygdala. That neurological structure plays a critical role in the impulse that startles us before the brain determines whether true danger is present. It sends the alarm at seeing a coiled rope before the executive sections of the brain determine it isn't a snake and issue an all-clear signal. Even though humans evolved greater functions, part of the nervous system, almost reptilian in its unemotional and nonanalytical drive for survival, is fearful and always on the lookout for danger, real or imagined, prehistoric or contemporary. It is suspected to be a prime source of modern-day anxiety and negative bias, seeing danger where none exists and exaggerating risk.

In the corporate world, I had been both predator and prey. Working in that universe, my amygdala was set to full throttle. I acted with aggression, even hostility, when I saw opportunities. When a large competitor aggressed, I fought intensely for a maximal outcome. Even when not in direct battle, I was always looking for a strategic advantage, just as any CEO should. But in the process, I lived with a constant rasp of anxiety because I was always on high alert, always on the lookout for hazards.

Fear wasn't all bad. While giving free rein to fear almost never led to a good outcome, letting it inform decision-making was critical to sound judgment. In *Descartes' Error*, neuroscientist Antonio Damasio was one of the first to point out the role of emotion in informing sound judgment. When a decision appears to be reasoned and rational but nonetheless evokes fear, it's ill advised to ignore the inner voice that signals alarm and cautions that something's not quite right.

Fear also could be the midwife of virtue because without fear, there could be no courage. When others told me I was courageous for taking a sabbatical, it was because they recognized the career risk I was taking and, with that, all the doomsday scenarios the mind can conjure. And yet, at some level, they recognized the benefit of leaning into the fear in order to cultivate the greater value of courage.

Now in Sumatra, in the face of real potential danger, I was plainly nervous. Even if I had wanted to turn back, there was no possibility of it because night was falling and travel to and from the village needed to be carefully coordinated. We were going to spend at least the night.

We strolled down a short walkway to Yusri Café and ordered our Indo standby, *nasi goreng*, vegetable fried rice, which was greasier and saltier than I would have liked. The power generators shut down early, and we had barely an hour after dinner to brush our teeth and get organized for bed. I took the porter's advice and sent the girls upstairs. We all relied on book lights for reading and got an early night's sleep.

In the morning, our guide picked us up after breakfast at Yusri Café. The air was fresh and the sky a clear cerulean blue. Amin took us across the river by open riverboat to the national park entrance and a feeding station where rangers cared for some of the semiwild orangutans. From there we went with Amin directly into the jungle to look for wild orangutans. About one hour into our trek, we hadn't seen a single animal. Amin said, "Stay here. I'll go ahead to see if I can attract an orangutan."

We sat on a downed log and snacked on food we'd brought with us. After about fifteen minutes, alone with my children in the middle of a jungle, I became increasingly aware of our solitude in the thick brush. The trails were unmarked, my cell phone screen showed "No Service," and our guide had disappeared. It was just three children, a vast jungle, and me. There went my brain again, responding not to imagined dangers but to real ones, not to the industrial predators that used to worry me at work but to natural ones like the snakes, tigers, and rhinos of the Sumatran jungle.

I looked for movement in the bush, which seemed serene enough. I called out to Amin. Nothing. I called out again. After about thirty long minutes, just when I was about to completely freak out, he showed up out of nowhere. "Come this way," he cheerfully said in his thick Indonesian accent. He pointed to a rustling in a tree about five hundred feet away. I looked up to find a large orange giant of an ape swinging slowly through the branches toward us. Though she seemed to lumber along, she covered the distance in about fifteen seconds. She stopped at a branch just overhead and made herself comfortable.

"Always keep five meters between you and the orangutan," Amin said. "If she gets too close, back away slowly and calmly." The orangutan lounged on that branch, eating whatever she had grabbed along the way, and just watched us with seeming disinterest. The sheer mass of that wild animal and its humanlike face left me breathless. Rita whispered under her breath, "Whoa! That is so cool." Nava started to imitate Amin's faux mating call, placing her palm at her mouth and kissing it loudly. Amin asked her to cut it out. I knew Nava was dying to feed the animal, but that would be too dangerous.

Eventually the orangutan moved on. We continued hiking deeper into the rainforest and stopped for lunch along a creek.

I asked Nava how she was holding up. We had been hiking for more than three hours. She said she was tired, and I told Amin it was time to head back.

As we started for home, I felt a raindrop, and then another, until a steady rain developed. The tracks slowly muddied, and our clothes dampened. After about an hour, Nava said she couldn't walk anymore. She just gave up as seven-year-olds do. I put her on my shoulders, and we carried on. When we had to clamber down a muddy slope, Amin and I passed Nava back and forth.

By the time we returned to Bukit Lawang after some six hours in the jungle, the rain had become a fierce downpour. The Bohorok River, which was fast on a sunny day, was beginning to rage. I remembered what I had heard about the river flooding, and this time, I kept my eye on the distance between our bungalow and the riverbank.

The rainstorm continued. The palm fronds outside our bungalow whipped in the wind. I grew increasingly uneasy. I looked for the manager of the bungalow but couldn't find him. When I asked at the café about him, they said he had left for Medan. He seemed to have hightailed it out of town. There was nobody else to talk to about whether or not the rainfall was dangerous and what to do about it. The rain became ferocious, and so did the river.

At dinner, Yusri Café was nearly empty. In the middle of our meal, the electricity went out, and we ate by candlelight. When I asked a couple of locals if they thought the rainwater was potentially dangerous, they just shrugged. My inner alarm system was blaring at full volume.

I decided to move all of us to the upper level of the bungalow. Even Nava pitched in to help move the mattresses from below to the level above. The kids didn't have trouble falling asleep, but I kept watch, listening to the rain and river below. Even as I tried to calm myself by focusing on my breath, as I'd trained myself in so-called calm-abiding meditation, my imagination ran wild.

The place had none of the safeguards I was used to in the West. There was no one and nothing to protect us, no one and no way to call for help. It was every person for him- or herself around here. I grew tired, and in time, I too fell asleep.

In the morning's early hours, the rain tapered off, and by the time the sun rose, the clouds had cleared. I looked out the window to see the river's edge at a safe distance. I felt the tension deflate, but I couldn't remember the last time I'd felt so unsafe.

I decided I'd incorrectly assessed the risks of visiting that rainforest, especially with young children. In businesses, I often weighed risks and benefits to make what I hoped were clear-headed decisions but always left a cushion for error, which I thought was a hallmark of sound judgment. "If you were to distill the secret of sound investment into three words," wrote the legendary investor Ben Graham, "we venture the motto, MARGIN OF SAFETY."

I didn't know if we were ever in any serious danger during our trip to Bukit Lawang, because nothing bad resulted. But I'd misjudged the risk, and the cost of getting it wrong wouldn't have been monetary but loss of life and limb. No meditation would help if things went the wrong way.

It was not my finest parenting hour. Victoria certainly would have been more sensible.

That day, the sun beat down hard. Moisture rose from the ground below, thickening the air with humidity that was almost solid. From our bungalow, we could see a pair of orangutans sunning themselves on a boulder by the riverbank. We stayed out of the jungle and flopped around in inner tubes in a slower part of the river.

We returned to our bungalow by midafternoon, sopping wet. As Nava waited her turn for a warm shower, she shrieked and pointed to the porch outside. At least a half-dozen monkeys had gathered and whooped outside. Sam grabbed a towel and bolted from the shower. Rita and Nava had already closed the door and were watching from the window. While the kids made faces at the animals, the monkeys ravaged a tube of Pringles we'd left outside, urinated on our drying clothes, and made off with Sam's flip-flops.

On our way home, during the ten-minute hike from Bukit Lawang to the road where we would meet our car, Sam and Nava paused to put together another animal report video for her friends back home. Sam sported two-dollar flip-flops we bought at a local *warung*. Nava's two front teeth, which had fallen out to reveal a stylish gap in her first video report from Africa, had grown back in and were visible as she filed her report for her class back home.

A few days after we arrived back in Bali, I went to a drawing session at Pranoto's gallery. I saw my friend Leo there and told him about our trip to Sumatra and specifically about the fear I'd felt. "The orangutans were beautiful," I said, "and my kids had a great time. But honestly, I felt really unsafe."

Leo had lived in Indonesia for years, and his naked response surprised me. "That's because Sumatra *is* unsafe."

seventeen

I t was late March when, once again, I prepared to sit in meditation. I was beyond thinking that meditation was a curious science experiment. What had started as a passing interest in the intersection of brain plasticity and Buddhist philosophy had blossomed into a serious undertaking. It had once been awkward to sit in silence. Now it was a sober attempt to retune my brain, quiet my nerves, and cultivate positive emotions like optimism, joy, compassion, and altruism.

I took a cushion from the house and dropped it on the gazebo's hardwood floor, just out of view of the back patio. The giant maroon blossoms and emerald leaves of the banana plant in our backyard obscured the water that rushed from the spring just beyond the property. I lit a stick of incense and placed it on the floor about three feet in front of me. Once it burned through, I would know my session was over.

I sat cross-legged on the cushion, the pyramid of my seat and legs forming a stable base upon which the rest of me rested. I felt the touch of cool air on my skin and took a deep breath. I set my intention: to change my thought patterns through meditation practice, crowding out natural aggression and feelings of competition with compassion and altruism.

Metta, or loving-kindness meditation, was a foundational practice of Buddhism used to cultivate benevolence by imagining altruism and locking it with silent phrase repetition. I started a bit like other meditation, by sitting and bringing awareness to the breath: the inhale, the exhale, and the negative spaces between them. I was now able to shift quickly into awareness. The shift was slight, subtle enough almost to be a nonshift.

Fragrant smoke from the incense wafted into my nostrils. I closed my eyes and relaxed them, letting them soften along with the rest of my body. I allowed my attention to fall on a few more deep breaths. I had nowhere to go and nothing to do. There was no agenda, goals, or expectations other than to be fully present at that time and in that place.

As the rhythm of my breathing steadied, I focused my attention on the fullness of each breath, one after another, sensing them as they began in the diaphragm and progressed to fill my lungs. I felt my chest and abdomen rise with each inhalation and slowly fall through each exhalation. I paid close attention to the breath, noticing which nostril predominated as air entered and left my body.

Many minutes passed like that, breath after breath, until I expanded my attention to my surroundings, allowing the sensation of the breath to fade slightly into the background. With my eyes still closed, I listened to the sounds around me. A Hindu priest chanted at the nearby village temple, his supplicant voice soaring. In the distance, a musician hammered away at metal bars, playing gamelan. Crickets chirped and birds warbled. An airplane flew overhead, its jets eclipsing the natural sounds of my immediate surroundings. I tried not to locate the plane in the sky or to express a dislike for the overpowering roar. I simply accepted the sound for what it was, letting it arise in my awareness, stay for a while, and disappear.

I returned my attention to the sound of my breath and then to the space between the breaths. In that empty silence, I noticed more sounds around me—a dog barking, a rooster crowing, a motorcycle driving by—until the sound of my next breath drew my attention again. From my drawing practice, I was increasingly sensitive to negative spaces. They had a way of enhancing perception and clarifying things. I noticed not just the space between shapes in a composition but also the silence between breaths. I saw my sabbatical as a negative space between professional challenges.

My mind wandered to an email I needed to write. I chased that thought for a while until I noticed that my attention had drifted. I brought it back to my breath. Then my mind wandered again as I thought of yet another mundane item, rehashing a conversation I'd had. Again, I noticed the wandering and refocused on my breath. Like that, I let my thoughts come and go, like the sounds around me, without engaging or judging them, simply observing, over and over again.

I felt the urge to scratch an itch on my right cheek. I didn't react. My neural system didn't necessarily work the way I'd been taught in school—that, in an infinitesimal instant, a neural message traveled from my cheek to my brain (itch), then from my brain to my hand (scratch). I knew now that between those two steps, the brain processed the information. There was room for the brain to fill in or to make things up entirely. By slowing down the process through meditation, by creating space, I could catch the impulse, slow it down, and quiet it. Instead of reaching for my cheek, I responded to the sensation by noting it and then focusing the laser beam of my attention on it. Magically, that simple act of bringing the itch from the periphery of my awareness to center stage melted the urge away. I returned my attention to my breath. I sat, surrendered in perfect stillness, feeling strength in the silence.

I entered another zone and felt myself drift off. I felt the peace of being in that single moment, and from that moment to the next. I opened my eyes to regain my concentration and saw the incense candle on the floor, burnt about two-thirds of the way through. I focused my gaze on its red glow.

Then out of nowhere and with my guard down, a tsunami of rage crashed into my consciousness. The anger was both familiar and intense. I thought I'd put it behind me, but its vestige now ambushed my calm. This time, I did not allow myself to be carried away by its power or to indulge in some endless loop of rumination. Instead, I leaned into it. As with an uninvited guest, I accepted its presence and welcomed it knowing that it would soon be leaving my consciousness.

But instead of fading, the rage twisted to grief. I felt it as deeply as I could and let it stay as long as I could. And when I could hold it no longer, I bid it farewell. The moment felt like a catharsis. I imagined that I had passed through a portal to a new sort of peace.

After a few minutes of grounding myself, my father entered the center stage of my conscious mind. It had been nearly twenty years since he died, but I could feel his love and support for me as fresh as if he were sitting beside me—and the rage and grief I'd felt at his sudden death. I imagined one of our hugs, his embrace always lasting a few moments longer than mine. I felt an acceptance from him that I did not need to earn or strive for. With each breath, I imagined his voice. *May you experience peace and well-being. May you be protected and free from harm. May you have peace of mind.*

For a moment, I felt silly imagining those phrases in my mind, but fragments of language didn't matter. What was important was the emotion. It helped imprint memory on the brain and create strong neural connections to combat mindlessness and disquiet. Breathing in his unconditional love and support was a start at creating neural pathways that emphasized positive emotion. Before long, I shifted to language that emphasized self-compassion: *May I experience peace and well-being. May I be protected and free from harm. May I have peace of mind.* I repeated the phrases over and over again, not mindlessly like a chant, but with full awareness and wholeheartedness. And again, I sensed my breath, the sounds around me, the sensation of my seat on the cushion.

Bathed in that loving kindness, I extended my field of compassion to include those closest to me, projecting rather than receiving kindheartedness. It was easiest to start with somebody I knew and loved naturally. I thought specifically about my children, especially Rita, who had suffered socially, and Oliver, still trying to gain his footing with new friends. I imagined draping them in fatherly love: *May you experience peace and well-being. May you be protected and free from harm. May you have peace of mind.* Lather, rinse, repeat.

My mind wandered. Struggling to maintain my concentration, I returned to the breath and the phrases and the emotions they evoked. From my children, I expanded my field of loving kindness to someone neutral and to whom I had no natural emotional connection. I thought about the men and women I had seen working the mines and fields around Ijen and about the imprisoned Bali Nine, broadcasting in my mind the *metta* phrase over and over again. *May you be protected and free from harm. May you have peace of mind.*

Finally, I thought of relationships that were difficult for me. My work relationships were many things, but they were not uncomplicated. In a world of intense competition, where often one person's gain came at another's expense, it was good to recognize everyone's common humanity and common desires to lead happy and fulfilling lives. We all were seeking the same things, no matter how we went about it. And as I sat there and wished it all for them—happiness, well-being, security—I felt the sense of competition and conflict deflate. In its place, openness and calm settled in.

In the distance, I heard Oliver and Rita bickering, the heat of their quarrel rising, as it sometimes did. I sank back into my zone, watching my thoughts as they passed through my awareness. I deliberately thought to cultivate compassion, first for myself, then others.

I sat in that state of mind for a while longer until I noticed the absence of any incense smell. I cracked my eyes open just a tiny bit to see that the incense stick had burned to its base and gone out. I looked at my watch. I had been sitting there for more than forty minutes, doing nothing but being aware of the texture of my surroundings, listening to the sound of my breath, and noticing the thoughts in my mind. It was not that I wasn't doing anything for forty minutes. I was simply being in that place and time, and that was everything.

Soon, I would end the meditation and stretch out my legs, and I would be back in the usual day-to-day. I knew that the practice of meditation, of falling back to awareness and observation of the conscious mind, took a long time to be effective, but ultimately, slowly, my mindset would shift.

I took in one last deep breath and extended my legs. I felt a stillness in my mind and a sense of peace. Through the mental gestures of loving kindness, I was able to let go of rancor and felt a joy of being alive. I gave my legs a few moments to adjust and work out the tingling before I stood. From the house, the bickering had escalated into something fierce. "Where's Daddy?" Rita shouted.

I lifted the cushion from the floor and headed back into the house. I'd have to break the kids apart, but I didn't tense up at the prospect. Perhaps one day they would outgrow their conflict. I didn't need to get caught up in the drama, but perhaps I could help defuse it.

eighteen | ᘈᘍᘈ

A week or so later, I met Karel for lunch. He was a tall man about my age sporting neatly cut hair, a former partner at McKinsey, the leading global management-consulting firm, which would be hard to deduce from his loose tropical clothing and soft, boyish looks. When I first met him, I had asked him why he had come to Bali. He said his fourteen-year-old son needed him, and he couldn't be present for him while traveling relentlessly to client meetings. He did not offer more about it, only that he chose his family over his grueling work schedule. He put his son into Green School as part of a plan to rededicate himself to his family and reset his priorities.

When it came to corporate careers, I felt Karel and I understood each other. He was an accomplished and thoughtful professional who could navigate his way through any business situation or organization. Now past the halfway point of our sabbatical, I was thinking about how I would handle returning home to my job.

We had arranged to meet at Clear Café on Hanuman Street. It wasn't a fancy place, but its architecture was an expression of the Ubud vernacular: yogi chic decor and fresh organic food. A wide convex staircase strewn with flower petals and tea candles led to the restaurant's entrance. Carved Indonesian hardwood framed the entranceway. An attendant exchanged my shoes for a claim check, just as an out-of-work actress in New York would do for a coat. She added my shoes to a jumbled pile.

Karel waited for me at a low-slung table made of lava stone. He sat cross-legged and upright on a cushion, the way many other patrons did. Months of practice at Yoga Barn had changed the way his large body could sit and move. When I joined him, a waitress came by and took our orders. I had my favorites, a fruit elixir made with local turmeric and a spicy green papaya salad.

He had recently returned to the Czech Republic to interview for his next gig. Among the opportunities he was exploring was the CEO position at a promising biotech company he was excited about. He thought the work was serious and engaging and promised real financial upside.

I was beginning to think about ways I could engage in my career and still maintain the sense of abundance I had in Bali. I had recently read *Flourish* by Martin Seligman, a University of Pennsylvania researcher and founder of an academic field called positive psychology. His earlier book was an instruction manual on raising children to be optimists because, he posited, raising optimistic children was akin to inoculating them against adult depression. It had helped Victoria and me with Oliver.

As a young child, Oliver often returned from school with stories that were variations on the same theme: "Everything bad always happens to me." Victoria and I followed Seligman's advice and reminded Oliver, whenever he recounted a vignette with that theme, that what happens in the course of the day is not pervasive, personal, or permanent. Sometimes good things happen, sometimes bad. Sometimes they happen to you, sometimes to others. And nothing is forever.

When the brain is young, it is most plastic and able to change. By following Seligman's advice, we attempted to recalibrate Oliver's negative bias, which was natural enough—everyone has a default set point on the spectrum of optimism and pessimism—but would not serve him well in adulthood. We were striving for something more positive. Over the course of time, we saw real changes in Oliver.

Now Seligman had advice for me. He sought to define a concept of an adult life of well-being and developed a checklist that went under the acronym of PERMA: Positive emotion, Engagement, Relationships, Meaning, and Achievement. I felt I'd recently made good progress on most fronts, especially through deliberate cultivation of positive emotion and relationships. But the concept of meaning eluded me.

"Don't you get enough meaning by providing for your family?" Karel asked.

"At some point I did. Now I'm not so sure. My career definitely *engages* me. And I get a buzz from *achievement*. In fact, I crave it. But *meaning*? I don't know."

"Well, what do you think about *meaning*?"

"I think it depends on circumstances. It's so broad and personal. I have to say, though, I'm inspired by what the Hardys are trying to do with Green School—not that it doesn't have its problems, but something about the vision, both a little out of reach yet still motivating. Not just its commitment to progressive education and global citizenship and all that but also a general push toward a greater good."

"Maybe you can find a cause you care about. Something that serves others. You don't have to find that kind of meaning in your job. You have to find it in your life."

I chewed on my salad and contemplated that for a moment.

"Anyway," he said, "you headed back to the same old life, or has something fundamentally changed? What are you thinking about for a job?"

"You just flew halfway around the planet for a bunch of job interviews. My focus right now is on being still—just *being*—for a few months."

"And what about *doing*? You still have to work, don't you?"

The synthesis of *being* and *doing* was simple in theory but difficult in practice. In fact, it was the fundamental challenge I was facing. After *doing* for so long in my career and *being* on my sabbatical, I would have to find a way to simultaneously keep my sense of awakening and be productive in the world.

"There are worse things than being a partner in an investment firm," I said. "The partners are smart. The work is interesting. It pays well. How bad could it be?"

Karel sipped his cashew milk chai latte. "You don't sound convinced."

"I have a new perspective on things. I can now deal with the mind-traps of that kind of life." I sensed he still wasn't buying it. "I just need to get my mojo back."

The waitress came by with the check.

"Mojo?"

"Swagger. I need to get excited about it again."

"Oh, you'll get that back once you return," he said as we fished for a few thousand rupiah to pay for lunch. He did not sound convinced. Here was a management consultant whose clients paid good money for strategic advice. He probably saw me as someone who did not have a fully formulated strategy.

On the way out, we handed our claim checks to the woman at the front door, who couldn't find our shoes. Eventually, Karel and I found them ourselves. We both needed to head to Green School for pickup, and I wanted to watch my kids play in an after-school Ultimate Frisbee match. My kids and Peter were the only ones who knew the game prior to our arrival in Bali. They not only taught the other kids and parents but organized regular competitive matches. I loved watching kids from all over the world—especially the Indonesians—toss a disc on Green School's large soccer field.

We mounted our motorbikes. "You know," I said, "I often advise colleagues never to burn bridges. But lately I'm wondering if some bridges need to be burned. Everything has its natural life cycle. Perhaps it's time let go and move on."

∿

That evening, Victoria received another phone call from her organization. This one seemed quieter and calmer. After it ended, she sat silently with the phone in her lap. After a minute or two, she let out a deep breath. "At last," she said. "The board decided to make a change to professional leadership."

"That's great," I said, hoping I was reading the signs right.

She smiled. "It finally sank in I wasn't coming back and JCP needed to be self-sustaining."

For the first time on the trip, she looked truly relaxed.

nineteen ᭣ᬯᬶᬰ

A few weeks later, Victoria and I drove our motorbike to the Purist Hotel outside Ubud. We pulled into the parking area, removed our helmets, and locked them to the bike the way Nyoman had showed us, placing the chinstraps into the locking mechanism of the saddle, securing them into place, and turning the key. We walked down a narrow footpath to the lobby to meet friends visiting from Chicago. Eric and Sharon had arrived in Ubud with their three children the day before. I smiled at how utterly worn our clothes looked compared to the crisp tops and bottoms they'd just unpacked. Our white shirts had turned gray from laundering in Bali's water and local detergent. I never reached lower than three layers down my clothing pile because Putu laundered daily. Neither Victoria nor I had cut our hair since the fall. Our clothes and hair were on sabbatical too.

After hugs all around, Victoria got down to business. "We've got a full itinerary for you guys. Whitewater rafting, biking, ropes course. And temples, lots of temples." She caught the eye roll from Matthew, their oldest. "Don't worry," she said. "There'll be lots of downtime." One thing we'd learned about traveling abroad with children was to reserve a few hours each day for nothing but play or splashing around in a pool.

I was eager to talk to Eric privately. He and I were both curious about meditation, Buddhist philosophy, and living in a way that he called "conscious." We were equally surprised by the hold that something as obscure as Eastern philosophy could have on us.

Yet Eric was on a special journey. Through meditation and other practices, he consciously set about to develop neural connections that promoted positive emotions, personal relationships, and a sense of abundance in his life. His mantra was *notice, shift, rewire.* First, notice negative thoughts as they occur, then shift them into something more positive to rewire synaptic connections. He meant that through meditation and by deliberately shifting thoughts from negative to positive, a sense of joy could be permanently etched into the brain. "Happiness is a teachable mental skill. It's a matter of training your brain," he said. "It's an inside job."

One morning during their stay, Eric borrowed Victoria's mountain bike, and he and I headed for Green School in a race to beat Nyoman and the kids. They had the benefit of the car, but we had the ability to skirt through traffic. Plus, we gave ourselves a head start.

As we set out at seven o'clock in the morning, the air was still cool, and the road to town was inked by morning shade. We cycled out of their hotel toward the center of Ubud. I played tour guide and pointed out a lavishly ornamented effigy of a black-and-gold bull under construction in the courtyard of the Royal Palace, just across the street from the central market on Jalan Raya. It was two stories tall and being prepared for a traditional cremation ceremony that would incinerate both the bull and the body entombed in it in a great ball of flame.

We turned down Hanuman Street toward Monkey Forest. The monkeys in the park were already hungrily searching for food. A few of them blocked our path but screeched and quickly scampered out of the way as we cycled on.

Eric asked, "How are you feeling about going back to work?"

"I don't know. I don't think about it much, but when I do, the thing I'm curious about is how to keep this sense of peace while competing in the world. I wonder if I'll have lost my edge or somehow gotten weak."

Eric's response was quick. "You've taken a giant step. You've assumed responsibility for the course of your life. You're not clinging to habits to secure your sense of self. That's strength, not weakness. That's big, big strength." He was complimenting me, but as if from a higher plane of wisdom.

We weaved our way through the narrow streets of Nyuh Kuning.

"The thing is," he said, "ambition for ambition's sake doesn't provide meaning or anything larger to frame your work." He had a brain-science explanation for every human behavior. "With each success, your brain gets a dopamine hit. You begin to crave it and find yourself just wanting more. But it's never enough. And anyway, it's a sugar high. It doesn't last."

This rang true. What had bothered me about striving was that it just led to more striving in the way that wanting just led to more wanting. I was constantly trying to push myself to greater achievement. It worked for a long time, but somewhere along the way, it no longer did.

We cycled down a trail that wound its way behind the John Hardy jewelry factory. I was preoccupied by our conversation when we turned a corner and heard the clanging of a gamelan. Before we knew it, we were amid a village ceremonial procession that blocked our way. A line of about thirty smiling Balinese women in sarongs, sashes, and lace tops carried towers of fresh fruit on their heads in devotional offering. Next to them, men in smaller numbers carried ceremonial parasols. They filed past as they made their way to the local temple. We dismounted our bikes, returned their smiles, and waited for them to pass. I had seen these ceremonies many times, but they still brought me joy.

"As for losing your edge," Eric said, "I think that warrants a little inquiry practice."

"What's that?"

"Most people actually believe their own thoughts. But thoughts are not facts. They're just thoughts. They don't necessarily reflect reality. Whenever you hear your inner voice saying, 'I haven't achieved enough,' or 'I don't have what it takes,' or whatever—and we all have that inner voice—ask yourself this: 'Is it true?' We're all attached to our stories, but it's worth asking coldly, 'What evidence do you have to prove beyond doubt that it's true?'" He suggested I ruthlessly apply the Socratic method to the judgmental opinions of my own mind. "If you can't find that evidence—because guess what? Most of the time it doesn't exist—then imagine how you'd feel if you told yourself a different story or simply envisioned yourself without that self-critical thought."

Okay, he was right. I'd engaged in my fair share of that kind of thinking before I left on sabbatical. Why not subject my thoughts to the same discipline and analysis that business decisions required? How did I know what I thought I knew? Where was the data?

Inquiry was a meditation of sorts; thoughts, not circumstances, had the power to inflict suffering. The sense of dissatisfaction was an illusion of the mind. Like meditation, the first step to overcoming negative thoughts was being conscious of them, to see them the way a meditator sees them and witness them from afar.

"You'll see when you get back to the US. Everybody compares themselves to others. They focus less on absolute achievement and more on achievement relative to their friends or whoever happens to be in the business press. It's a negative thought stream that's a recipe for unending suffering."

I knew what he meant. Back in New York, try as I might to fight it, I often compared how I was doing relative to others. When I did, I tried to remember another lesson from rowing. I'd hear the voice of my school rowing coach bellowing from the riverbank: "Keep your eyes in your own boat!" Diverting my

attention from what was happening in my own shell to the racing eight next to me was a sure strategy for failure, especially as
we pushed to the finish. I knew comparing was an unwinnable
race. Still, it took energy to fight the impulse.

Eric said, "You know that self-critical voice that you—and
everyone else—have? Think about this: Would you ever let yourself talk to anybody else as harshly as you talk to yourself?"

"Got any reading materials to recommend?" I asked.

"Anything by Byron Katie," Eric said. "*A Thousand Names for
Joy* is the best self-help book there is. You're going to love, love,
love what she has to say."

When the procession passed, I looked at my watch, mindful
of the time and the contest. We needed to pick up the pace. We
cycled past the Aqua water-filtration plant, over a bridge that
spanned the Ayung River, and down a road that headed toward
the village of Mambal.

I called out, "You up for a shortcut?" Before Eric had a chance
to respond, I led us off the main road and down to a grassy
path that ran by a wide canal. From there, the trail led through
thick tropical brush and narrowed to a thin ribbon of rocky soil.
By now, I'd gotten used to these Balinese bike tracks.

About half a kilometer along, another trail broke off to the
left in a straight line up a steep incline. We took it. My rear wheel
spun, but I quickly regained traction by shifting my weight far-
ther back on the bike. Eric was right behind me.

We came upon a clearing where the foundation of a new villa
was being built. Freshly cut trees and foliage lay on the ground. A
deep, wide swath of ochre soil lay bare in the bright tropical light.
The Green School's environmental agenda was having its impact
on me, and I was momentarily saddened by the wound in the
earth and the loss of jungle to make room for yet another villa.
Construction seemed to be picking up, and with Bali having little
in the way of zoning laws, it threatened the island's greenery.

We cycled for another fifteen minutes, talking more about
self-inquiry. We reached the school entrance just ahead of

Nyoman and the kids. Asher smiled and waved from behind his counter at the *warung*. "Coffee?"

We spent the morning touring Green School and Green Village, another Hardy project, a community of high-end homes, made of bamboo and other sustainable materials that were architecturally no less magnificent than the school's buildings. The homes spiraled from the verdant ground to float above the canopy and overlook a terraced ravine that led to the Ayung River.

As we exited Green Village on a footpath, I asked Eric if he ever considered taking some extended time off. He paused for a moment to consider the question. He shrugged nonchalantly. "My life's a sabbatical." I observed my spasm of competitiveness and annoyance. It quickly evaporated, and I chuckled to myself.

〰

On a morning I planned to spend drawing at Pranoto's, Eric and Sharon borrowed our motorbike and dropped me off at the studio. It wasn't legal to have three on a bike, but having seen local families hang as many as seven on a single bike, I pushed it. They motored off to the wholesale shopping road near Tegalalang in search of small mementos. Instead they found a life-sized standing stone Buddha that was so large and heavy, it had to be shipped back to Chicago by marine cargo.

When they returned to the villa later in the day, I needed the bike to pick up Nava from a playdate in Sayan, on the other side of Ubud. Eric asked to join. He sat on the back of the bike, and when we picked up Nava, she sat between my legs on the front of the bike's saddle. "Nava!" I yelled over the bike's motor. "Sing 'Living in Bali' for Eric!" She immediately launched into it, belting out her school's spirit song.

> *Living in Bali*
> *We know where we're going.*
> *Our river is flowing,*
> *The current is strong.*

The light in our eyes
Is the place we believe in
Destiny's weaving.
It guides us along.

Living in Bali
The island's life giver,
The great Ayung River,
Flashes and darts,
Carries our hope
From the hills to the ocean,
A powerful motion
That strengthens our hearts.

Hey! Hey ya—a—a!
This is who we are.
Hey hey hey ya—a—a!
Living in the heart of Indonesia.

Our families spent the next few days together, adventuring, splashing, talking, and eating. "Our kids are infatuated with yours," Sharon said to me. I thought the feeling was mutual. The unacknowledged and good-natured rivalry between Eric and me, I realized, enhanced the learning experience.

twenty | ぴo

In mid-April, Oliver returned from his Summit to Sea outing. The theme of Oliver's field trip was water's fundamental role in biodiversity, and he spoke excitedly as he told us about it. He had hiked to a thundering waterfall and, along the way, collected water samples from mountain streams. As monkeys observed him and his classmates from their overhead perches, he had picked his way through mangroves looking for mud samples to view under a magnifying glass. He had traveled by motorized *jukung*, a small wooden Indonesian outrigger canoe, to snorkel over a coral reef in the warm waters of the Bali Sea. He was on a total high from the experience. I wondered if his joy on this excursion stemmed from something similar to his love of team sports.

He returned home just as we were preparing for the Passover holiday's festive meal, the Seder. We had invited our friends into our home to celebrate with us. My brother, who lived in Israel, would also join with his family. In New York, an invitation like that was commonplace, and many non-Jews attended them. In Bali, a Seder was a rare thing. Most of our friends had never participated in one, and our invitation quickly became a hot ticket.

The story of Passover is one of ancient redemption, of a mass exodus from slavery to freedom. But contemporary celebration had evolved to commemorate political, social, and personal redemptions of all stripes. On this equatorial island, we were surrounded and enveloped by people who had searched in one way or another for their own personal redemption and, like the Israelites, had simply picked up and left where they'd come from to arrive in a foreign land. Many had interesting stories to tell. Since one of the traditions of the Seder is to tell the story of redemption, it was the perfect setting for people to open up and share, even if it made them feel vulnerable.

We decked out our pad, incorporating Balinese culture and sensibility into our own traditions. We hired a small catering group to cook traditional Balinese fare while observing the special dietary restrictions of Passover. The group strewed vibrantly colored flower petals on the floors at the entrance of our home, and in the dining area, they served food on banana leaves in bamboo trays. We sat on floor cushions, Bali style, around lowslung tables. Throughout the property, Nyoman placed devotional offerings filled with incense and bits of food. Attire was Bali formal. For women, that meant a lacy blouse, sarong, and a sash tied over the top; for men, a white shirt and sarong. Balinese headdress was optional, but I wore a yarmulke.

The script, guide, and liturgy of the evening were laid out in the *Haggadah*, an ancient text, the bulk of which was recited before the festive meal. It could take hours to plow through. I didn't want to torture the uninitiated with a drawn-out affair and was prepared to move things along quickly. But over the course of the service, each time I tried to rush, someone objected. Our guests were utterly curious and engaged, and they wanted more.

Sam especially wanted to keep it authentic. He and the other children had an opportunity to explain their own culture and respond to our guests' questions. It made our kids feel special and built confidence in their own identities. They never had to describe their identities to anyone in New York; it was part of the air they breathed. They sometimes felt awkward keeping kosher at Green School, but now they felt proud.

As we progressed, some of our guests related their search for personal redemption. We knew their individual stories from vignettes we shared during mountain-bike rides or talks over a fresh coconut at the Green School's *warung*. Bali attracted men and women who journeyed through their own personal wilderness. Some, like the ancient Israelites, were wanderers, although our guests were nomadic by choice and relished the excitement of living in new places. Others sought the spirituality and joy of the island, its beauty, and its complex, animistic culture. Still others had come to fix a troubled marriage, recover from a recent divorce, or deal with addiction. Many were simply burnt out from jobs or relationships that weren't working.

Nobody found coming to Bali easy. The move invariably required courage to leave comforts of the familiar for the risk and promise of imagined deliverance. Most had to sacrifice something important to be on that island. They often left their extended families behind. For highly personal reasons, each had made a deliberate choice to live life differently than his or her peers, to live it as he or she wanted. Each found the bold choices to be empowering. Everyone had a story about why they'd pulled themselves out of the game and readily placed their cards, face up, on the table. If they hadn't yet found redemption in Bali, they were certainly seeking it.

Sometimes their narrative involved something to do with work, but usually that was only a superficial element. Underneath, something was often going on in their personal or family lives. Some were escaping, others had come to reconnect with their immediate families, and still others were stretched too thin financially. One friend had mentally ill family members, and it was beyond his capacity to take care of them. If he'd tried, he believed he would have been swallowed whole. Living in Bali, even while making frequent trips home, was his way of coping.

That evening, our friends shared their stories without sugarcoating them. Vulnerability and tears were accepted. It was striking that nobody judged anybody else or tried to peg them on the socioeconomic ladder.

I too opened up. I told the story of my journey, my own search for redemption. Some of my relationships back home were troubling me, and despite my love and admiration for those people, perhaps I needed to change or shed the relationships. I wanted to refocus my priorities away from money, status, and title and recommit to my personal relationships, particularly my family, which had lacked my presence for too long. I needed a break from being driven by ambition and ego. I pulled at the hem of routine to refocus on creativity. And while I sought to still my stirring ego in order to live with greater compassion and gratitude, I wondered if, at the same time, it was possible also to engage fiercely and wholeheartedly. Could *anyone* live a harmonious and balanced life and simultaneously achieve great success?

I paused for a moment. Was I making Victoria or the kids uncomfortable with my confessional? Victoria gave me a warm smile. Sam raised his eyebrows as if telling me to get on with it. Oliver was inscrutable. Rita seemed deep in thought. Nava was fiddling with something on the table. At least none of my family looked horrified or mortified.

"I chose to make a change in my life and come here. But it was a choice I had a lot of help with." I looked at Victoria. "I had to be pushed." We smiled at each other and got a few laughs. "But after I got here, I chose to continue to change. I have a greater sense of personal power—or maybe responsibility is a better word—from making a thoughtful choice. To deliberately cultivate a sense of happiness and not allow myself to be carried along by the currents of my life or to be a slave to it." I quietly acknowledged, as if to convince nobody but myself, the temporary nature of our stay in Bali and that permanent escape was not redemption and certainly not a viable strategy even if the fantasy was tempting.

I read a poem by David Whyte, self-proclaimed poet laureate to the corporate world. Whyte generally wrote about the self in the context of family and work, and especially about navigating the waters of extraordinary experience, fierce engagement, and turning points. His leitmotif was wholeheartedness, and he published "Fire in the Earth," a poem that spoke to me. In it, he evoked Moses at the burning bush. At one of his readings, as Whyte tells it, an Orthodox Jewish student approached and suggested to Whyte that the Hebrew verb that the Bible employs when God says to Moses, "Take off your shoes!" is the same verb that is used to describe an animal shedding its skin. As Moses passes into a new life—an utterly new existence from the one he has known—he needs first to shed, to molt, to remove the skin that no longer serves him in order to don a truer veneer.

In shedding my busy life, I seized the opportunity to reconnect with my ground of being, my ground of awareness. When I reconnected with important relationships, I realized that, like Whyte's Moses, I had been standing on holy ground all along. I needed to shed parts of an older life in order to reemerge into something new, even if I had yet to define what that was.

"I have struggled to let go of my ego, my sense of self being at the center of things. Why do we continuously attempt to fill our lives only with those things that we like and banish those that we don't? It's as if we stamp experience with 'like' and 'don't like' icons. Thumbs up, thumbs down." It all seemed like an endless path with no possible destination. I tried to let go, at least for a while, of my burning desire to succeed and realized that I didn't need more than I already had and that I could accept or deal with whatever came my way.

Although I knew there was a difference between redemption and escape, I had not resolved which applied to me. I considered that perhaps Bali was about neither escape nor redemption but simply renewal. If so, would my life really be different when I returned to New York?

The Seder lasted six hours, and the last guest left at one o'clock in the morning.

Poor Nava was bored by all the adult talk and half asleep by the time it was over. Rita seemed to bask in the peaceful gathering. Oliver, still buoyed by this recent expedition, said, "Wow, Daddy, this sabbatical is a big deal, isn't it?"

Sam listened raptly but had little to say until the next day. "I had no idea. It's like you're showing me how I should live my life."

♏

We woke late the next morning when the sun already hung high. My brother suggested we go for a walk through rice fields, which lay beyond the spring that ran behind our villa. We descended the steep steps, cut from local lava stone, and made sure to hold on to the handrail so as not to slip on the wet moss. Intricately carved stone spouts spit spring water from the hillside into the large stone stalls in which the locals bathed and collected water for their homes. We climbed the steps on the opposite side of the ravine. As we turned to stroll through a rice field, a boy carrying a towel smiled as he passed us on his way to bathe below.

I asked my brother, "Why go back to New York? Why don't I just stay? I'm as happy here as I've ever been." I was kidding around, but it suddenly hit me that it was true. A sense of impending loss settled over me.

I'd had many conversations with Victoria about lengthening our stay. Our time in Bali had been filled with moments of breathless joy, and like Cinderella, we wished we could dance a little while longer. The food tasted better. Sleep was deeper. Each day felt like a gift. I thought I'd discovered something profound. I connected to critical relationships in my life. I recognized that the basic needs, drives, and desires of people were all the same: they wanted to suffer less and enjoy more. I was grateful for what I had and didn't want more. For the first time in many, many years, I felt awake. Without being pulled simultaneously in multiple directions, I felt fully present in time and place.

"Easy for you to stay," my brother said, "but what about your kids? Bali isn't real life. What will they be equipped for when they wander out into the world?"

It took my brother to remind me that I had a responsibility to my children beyond spending time with them. First was to provide them with a strong education, the kind that was difficult to make up for once the time for it had passed. Victoria and I had bought into Green School's premise that a formal education designed to build a workforce for the industrial age may fade into irrelevance in a world of constant change, machine learning, artificial intelligence, and smart robots. Although our sabbatical was a priceless piece of education on its own, I was now thinking about formal education. Whether it was exposure to science, music, language, or sports, their lives were enhanced by the first-rate education available in New York City. If many families had come to Bali for six months and ended up staying for three years, other families left because the children weren't getting the education they needed or were falling behind in core educational subjects, at least as measured by commonly accepted standards. Being progressive and creative may be necessary, but I didn't think it was sufficient. And the value of being an educated individual lay far beyond acquiring any technical or creative skill.

Things began to sink in. I spoke to local friends too about the struggle we felt. Some of them were speechless at the notion of choosing the quality of our children's education over our own happiness. We understood it wasn't a simple trade-off between being happy and being unhappy. After all, we'd hardly been miserable in New York. We had to take a longer view.

I went home that night and told Victoria about my conversation. She reminded me—as if I need to be reminded—that we also had family back home. Our parents were already into their senior years. We needed to be around. The practicalities of life kept us from staying in Bali. If we stayed longer, I could imagine my partners losing patience with me, and I wouldn't have blamed them. While taking a sabbatical was normal to me now, I suspected that it still seemed wacky back home. And there was a natural limit to the length of a leave of absence. In any event, I was not prepared to sacrifice education and family in order to live as a modern-day lotus-eater.

In the end it was Sam who, at fifteen years old, was wise enough to bring it all home: "I want to stay too, but I know I need to go back." He was a good student and wanted to go to a good college. He knew his high school back home was equipped to prepare him for that goal and guide him. As exciting as Green School was, he needed something different from what it had to offer. And what was true for Sam was true for all of us. We wanted to stay but knew we had to return.

ᔕ

It was May, and our time in Bali was drawing to a close when Victoria and I traveled an hour to the village of Klungkung to visit another artist, Nyoman Gunarsa. Gunarsa was better known than Karja, more tied to traditional Balinese symbolism, and deeply committed to Bali's cultural heritage. Already in his seventies and walking with pain, Gunarsa gave us a tour of his studio and family compound. He led us through his own private museum of traditional Balinese artifacts and showed us a temple he was building for his family. But it was his paintings that we were mostly interested in, having seen many of them in Ubud's museums.

Gunarsa's works were colorful and lyrical. They depicted Balinese dancers and musicians that evoked rhythm and symmetry. He too was concerned with energy. He moved quickly and worked with bold colors. Sometimes he applied paint directly from the tube to the canvas. His figures and symbols were uniquely Balinese and in themselves devotional offerings. Often his paintings were framed in broad teak boards that he carved, again with Balinese figures and symbols, which became integral elements of his composition.

We spent almost an entire day with him. We liked a piece that he kept in his office. He was reluctant to sell us any of his pieces without his daughter, who was his business manager, but we prevailed and bought one that we knew would hang in the center of our apartment and be a constant reminder of our time in Bali.

Slowly, I was incorporating art into my life. Collecting these pieces might help me integrate the changes in my life that I was now experiencing into the New York life I would soon need to return to. I wondered if I was already moving back into a more materialistic way of living, of buying art rather than creating it. I promised myself to keep working on my own art whether or not Victoria and I bought accomplished pieces that truly moved one or both of us.

∿

When we returned home to meet the kids as they arrived from school, we saw that Sam, who had not been feeling well, was becoming very ill. We had thought that his headache and cough was a mere cold, but now he developed a fever. Over the next few days, he became very lethargic, had trouble getting out of bed, and had no appetite. At times, he was so weak, he couldn't sit up. Days passed, and he didn't improve. We took him to the medical clinic in Ubud and then to one in Denpasar, but nobody knew what the matter was. We took him to Green School's Dr. Ating, who thought it could be any number of things. Dr. Ating took some tests and a few days later emailed, "The results are difficult to interpret. Let's hope it's paratyphoid."

What we did know was that Sam was suffering and losing weight at an alarming rate, nearly 15 percent of his body weight in a little over one week. As the days wore on and he got sicker and sicker, Victoria and I grew very concerned. We were reaching our wits' end with medical guesses and conflicting opinions. I told Sam, after about ten days of this illness, that if he didn't recover within two days, I would take him to Singapore to seek more sophisticated medical attention.

As Sam slept one day, Victoria and I took our motorbike into town to run some quick errands. Victoria sat on the saddle behind me, hugging my chest for stability the way she normally did when we rode together. She let her head rest on the back of my shoulders.

Chickens screeched as we flew past. I yelled to be heard above the din of the engine. "I'm sick of the dogs and the chickens and the pollution. I'm tired of this third-world living. And I'm nervous about Sam. I'm ready to go home." Something about Sam's illness had caused me to see Bali in a different light. Like Junjugan's migrating herons, an internal instinct told me that it was time to move on, and I surrendered to our timeline.

When we returned to the villa, Sam was awake and said he was feeling a little better. We kept a close eye on his appetite and energy. Two days later, he turned a corner.

twenty-one | ᎯᏤᎧᎩ

I went to my final session at Pranoto's. In the previous few weeks, I had tried to draw something every day. Pranoto's studio was special to me, and drawing there had become a focal point of my experience in Bali. That day, I felt the weight of an ending.

Just as they always had been, the first two hours were an exercise in frustration as I struggled to get into R-Mode. At one of the breaks, I said to a fellow artist, Pranoto's daughter, who was visiting from Java, that I found drawing difficult. She took my hand and smiled. "It's difficult for all of us. That's why we do it."

It was more than difficulty that drew the artists to that room. Just as intention was important in yoga and meditation, it showed itself in art too. Without the artist's intention, art was worthless. The art critic Arthur Danto asks what the difference is, for example, between an original painting, say by Jackson Pollock, and a perfect replica of it. Or, in the reverse, what is the difference between Andy Warhol's replica of the Brillo boxes and the original boxes that were produced on an assembly line? Why is one worth millions of dollars while the identical item is worth next to nothing? They certainly look the same. One answer is intention. It is the artist's intention in an original work that simply can't be present in copies or frauds. The intention of the original boxes was commercial, but the intention of Warhol's was high art. He took a familiar object, set it in a new context, and made it special. It was his intention to stimulate curiosity in the viewer—to show us an object stripped of our automatic presumptions about it—that made it art. Conversely, the intention behind fraud makes forgeries less than worthless.

It is intention that stands at the doorstep of creation. It smells the freshness of the moment and brings to the world a new idea or perspective. As I continued to struggle with Seligman's notion of meaning's contribution to well-being, I recognized that without intention, there could be no meaning. Even if the main intention evident in a beginner's work like mine was to create a convincing likeness of a person or scene, once the technique was mastered, deeper meaning could emerge.

At Pranoto's, I counted five languages being spoken among the fifteen or so artists who sat on cushions and gathered around the model in the center of the room. During the breaks, some artists pulled out musical instruments. I listened to guitar, ukulele, and flute while the model stretched to relieve her muscles. I took a meditative moment to absorb the scene, to notice the good in order to rewire neural pathways and cultivate joy. In an alternate life, this could be my world.

Leo, the retired philosophy professor from Edinburgh, was at Pranoto's that day. I talked to him about his technique and the direction he was taking his art.

"I'm drawing only in ink now," he said.

"Why?"

"I like the sense of commitment."

I asked Leo how old he was. He blew my mind. "Eighty-six." I thought of the work of Ellen Langer from Harvard University, the early pioneer in the field of mindfulness. Much of her work had focused on mindfulness as it related to aging and how it positively affected men and women as they grew into their senior years. Here in front of me was a man on his way to ninety years old, looking fantastic and still learning and experimenting. Now at eighty-six, he was finally ready to commit.

The night before, Leo and I had attended a screening of the movie *Happy* at an expat community event. His example reminded me that the lessons from that film—that happiness is derived from pursuing intrinsic values, like love, gratitude, and courage, which connect us to one another—were first articulated thousands of years ago by Aristotle, who did not consider power, status, and money to be intrinsically valuable.

At the end of the drawing session, when I said good-bye to Leo, he gave me a drawing he'd made of me. Apparently he'd lost interest in the model at one of our sessions and turned his attention my way. Because I'd been so lost in concentration, I had no idea he was drawing me. I was touched by the gift. It made me feel I'd joined some fellowship of artists. I was also startled by my huge nose. Gifting his own art was a wonderful act of gratitude and generosity, something to which I could aspire when my drawing skills improved beyond novice. For a moment, I noticed familiar self-criticism—was my nose really that elephantine?—until I surrendered to what was.

After Leo left, I had a better look at the drawing. I loved being depicted as a true artist, drawing and yet at the same time meditating. I sighed. It was really me.

Afterward, I met Victoria at the Yellow Flower Café, a favorite of ours. I arrived early. While I waited for her, a waitress saw my drawing pad. "Been drawing, yah?" she asked in a thick Balinese accent.

I smiled. "Yes. Would you like to see?" I showed her what I was up to.

"Ah, *bagus bagus*," she said. "Very good. Still learning, yah?"

〽

As we prepared to wind up our time in Bali, Sam was invited to an end-of-year party with some friends on a Friday night. By that time, his friendships at school had solidified. Well into his teenage years, Sam yearned to spend more time with his friends and less with his family. Victoria and I told him what he already knew, that he could not attend a party on Shabbat.

He flew into a kind of rage I'd never seen before, stomping around, flinging his arms out, sputtering disjointed phrases. He was beside himself, not knowing what to do with his anger. He knew what Friday nights meant in our family, and the conflict was eating him up. He threatened to give up Shabbat as soon as he had gained his independence. Our other traditions, which he said he disdained, would suffer the same fate.

What he said didn't bother me, but it hurt to see him in such a state. I didn't know what to do for him. I also took a step back from my insistence and patriarchal authority to wonder if my decision was right. Should our family tradition preempt Sam's outward mobility, his urge or perhaps even his obligation to cross the boundaries he was brought up in and find his own way? Here was where Victoria and I often disagreed, less on the substance of the matter and more on degree. I tended on the side of self-exploration, she on the side of family and tradition.

I decided to distract and calm him down. He loved our motorbike, and I invited him to come along on it while I ran an errand. Victoria was happy for me to take charge. On the way home, he let loose a tirade and lashed out at everyone: Victoria, his sisters, and me. He did not even exempt Oliver, with whom he bonded tightly. He was tired of being told what to do and how to behave and—directed at his school back home—what to think. He was dying for his independence. He was struggling to synergize the joy of an open, creative education in Bali with the more formal and religious education to which he was going to return.

In our attempt to steep our children in their own culture while simultaneously engaging them in more global affairs, Victoria and I recognized the risk that they might find our restrictions claustrophobic or irrelevant. I understood Sam's conflict because I too yearned for an expansive world view based on being curious about and participating in the larger world while simultaneously maintaining ties to my culture, people, and faith. I told Sam that when he went to college, he would be free to make whatever life decisions he wanted. Nonetheless, I said, our family had chosen to live our lives in a certain way, and we intended to stay committed to it.

We headed home, and about half a kilometer from home, I pulled over and dismounted the bike. Sam had calmed down. Although he was only fifteen, I offered to let him drive the motorbike alone for the first time. I gave him a hug and started to walk home. Soon he accelerated past me. I hoped that in his life, he would do the same.

When I returned home, he was sequestered in his room. But when it was time to gather for Friday-night dinner, he sauntered out in his sarong, ready to join the family.

twenty-two

Classes at Green School ended in June. We hired a local shipping company to crate up the paintings we'd collected, about half a dozen pieces by local artists. Visiting museums, galleries, and artist studios had become Victoria's and my activity on most afternoons. We learned as much as we could. I was never too shy to ask artists questions about technique, theory, and intention. We were introduced to artists first by Richard, the friend who told us about Green School back in New York, and later by his friend Sika, another accomplished artist who had taught many others at the local School of Fine Arts. Some of these artists commanded rich prices by Balinese standards from collectors in Jakarta and elsewhere but still vastly less expensive than New York. Often, we visited artists in their family compounds and met their families and friends. Sometimes we were invited to remove our shoes and join them for a snack. There always seemed to be a chicken clucking its way around these places, and I smiled to myself at the thought that I never did get a chance to use my *chalef*.

One local artist lived ten minutes down the road from our villa. I noticed him working every time I drove by because his studio was open and faced the street. His style was familiar; it had a flat, primitive, modern sensibility. I asked Nyoman to join me for a visit so that he could help translate. I asked the artist if I could commission him to create a large painting from a photograph. When he agreed, we settled on a price.

Two weeks later, for Mother's Day, I presented Victoria with a gift. It was the artist's interpretation of a casual family photograph of the six of us the day in January when we bought and wore our first sarongs. I'd been self-conscious about that photograph because it was so at odds with the corporate image I had of myself, and I knew it would get distributed back home. Now not only was I comfortable with the image; I also celebrated it.

Over the next few days, we made sure to see our friends over dinners, parties, and picnics to say good-bye. By the time our last bag was packed, Rita said, "I wish we could stay another year. I'm really going to miss my friends here. I don't want to go back to New York."

But on Sunday morning, Nyoman came to pick us up to take us to the airport. He was dressed sharply, a rolled blue morning glory tucked behind his right ear. He hurried us along to make sure we wouldn't miss our flight. We rode to the airport mostly in silence. We passed familiar scenes, the rows of artisan shops that sold Bali-made bric-a-brac and Buddha statues and the surf stores of Kuta. Nava cried out, "Good-bye!" to each landmark. By the time we pulled into the airport drop-off zone, the car was thick with the sadness of our leaving. We were especially upset to leave Nyoman, but it was he who shed the tear. Bali had changed us, but I could see that in our own small way, through Nyoman, we had changed Bali too. And that had meaning for me.

As we waited for our flight, Rita asked me to record a song she wrote about Bali. The lyrics were in great contrast to the sad songs she wrote in Africa:

As I'm walking in Bali, I never feel alone,
  I hear the dogs barkin' and the ducks quackin'.

In this beautiful sunlight,
On this wonderful day,
And this beautiful sunshine
Is comin' my way.

As I'm walking through the rice,
I see the farmers wave
With a knife in their hand,
They're all over the land.

In this beautiful sunlight,
On this wonderful day,
And this beautiful sunshine
Is comin' my way.

There are temples, cremations, and offerings too,
Living in Bali for me is dream come true.

twenty-three

We planned to travel for six weeks through Southeast Asia as we slowly made our way home. Sam still hadn't regained all his weight from his bout with paratyphoid. He looked wan. Victoria tried one last time to change his mind about returning to camp for the summer. I braced myself for another dramatic episode.

Sam took a breath and looked at her. "Mommy, we talked about this before we left New York. I need some hang time with my friends before school starts." He clearly was ready to break from the intense time with his parents. They both looked at me.

The first leg of our journey home would be through Vietnam. The place held such an important place in American history and our collective psyche that I thought it was important for him to experience it. "How about coming with us to Vietnam and then heading off to camp?" I said.

He shrugged. "That's cool." And with that compromise, Victoria and I accepted that Sam would be moving on.

On Sam's final day with us, as we walked back to the hotel from our visit to the Hanoi Hilton, I asked Sam how he felt about leaving the family. He said he had mixed feelings. He was excited to see his friends back home and eager to get back to American food. But he was sad to leave his friends in Bali. It upset him to know that he was unlikely ever to see them again, at least for a long while.

"Leaving Bali sucks," he said. "It's the mood in the family we built up over the last few months. Now we're going back to our regular New York thing."

I knew exactly what he meant. How would we keep our sense of adventure going? How could we maintain our closeness once we reintegrated into the structures and responsibilities of work, school, and extended family? I didn't have good answers to those questions. "Can you carry the mood inside you?" We both knew it was a trite line.

"That'll be hard," he said. "The stress of school, all the work. I'll try."

When we arrived at the hotel, Victoria finished packing Sam's bags and closed them. We helped him bring them down to a waiting taxi. Sam said his farewells and hugged his siblings awkwardly. Victoria didn't tear up. Instead she focused, as she often did, on the list of things to be done, this time to ensure Sam arrived safely to her sister, Abigail, who would meet him at JFK. Then Sam and I climbed into the taxi bound for the airport.

As we talked in the car, I was struck by how mature his manner was, how much more adult his face had become, and how much he seemed to have grown. Nobody in our family saw more change from our sabbatical than Sam. Freed from the pressures of a New York private school, he shined. His sense of humor was like a jack-in-the-box, flying out suddenly from within to get a laugh. He engaged. He played. He created.

In Bali, Sam and I rediscovered each other. It was all so very earnest back home. Whether it was my work or his school, the stakes always seemed high. We ratcheted down the ante in our travels. We had breakfast and dinner together practically every day. I didn't have meetings, business travel, or conference calls. He didn't have too much homework.

By the last day of school, Sam had become so integrated, so woven into the fabric of the expat community in Bali that he surprised me—and, I think, himself—at how difficult it was for him to rip himself away. When I looked at a picture of him on my phone from when we left New York, I was astonished by the change in a few short months.

I walked Sam to the check-in counter. He was still so thin that he had trouble keeping his pants at his waist. His hair, normally close-cropped, had grown into a bush of wild curls. He wore flip-flops and carried an electric guitar case collaged with tourist stickers from places we'd been. By the looks of it, he had fully transitioned from Upper East Side prep-school kid to Bali hippie.

The airline representative at the counter smiled and took his passport. The trip to JFK by way of Seoul would take about twenty hours. She looked up from her computer at Sam. "You're fifteen years old?" She came around to our side of the counter and hung a large, bright-yellow ID around his neck that shouted in cute bubble letters, "Unaccompanied Minor," a reminder from the universe that Sam was not quite yet a man. Still, he was no longer a boy.

Sam and I walked together to the security checkpoint. He was a jumble of excitement, nerves, and adrenaline. Traveling alone over great distance was a coming-of-age moment for him and for me. Having matured so much in Bali, independent travel capped the sabbatical. I felt a swell of both sadness and pride as I gave him one last hug. And he was off. My boy was on his own.

Saying good-bye to Sam reminded me of the many times in college and later when my own father, also named Sam, saw me off at the airport. My father never appeared to me to struggle with his values and ideas of virtue. He found all of it in the divine. Just as I had done with my son, my father used our car rides to the airport to talk privately with me. Sometimes he broached a sensitive topic. Mostly, I figured, my mother had put him up to it. Either way, I'd always felt safe with my father because he was incredibly loyal and always had my back. The last of those conversations took place on the way to an airport only a few weeks before he died suddenly at the age of sixty-one. It was the last time I saw him.

ᴨ

From Vietnam, the rest of us traveled to the Buddhist temples and monasteries of Luang Probang in Laos, set high in the mountains at the confluence of the Khan and Mekong Rivers. There, each morning, hundreds of monks and their novices in saffron robes from the various monasteries walked through the streets collecting alms. The temple roofs gleamed amid overgrown hardwood trees; markets sold gorgeous silks of bright hues and intricate patterns.

On our first morning, I woke before dawn, when the first notes of birdsong rose from the hotel garden, to participate in the daily alms procession conducted by the monastery monks. I left the family asleep in their warm beds and walked toward the main street. I stopped by a small shop to buy some sticky rice so I could offer it as alms to the monks, then waited for them by a curb. They filed past, their heads shaven and their maroon-and-gold robes flowing against the backdrop of a dense morning mist. I sat on a damp sidewalk, took some rice with my fingers, and placed the food in their begging bowls. When I had no more rice to offer, I pulled out my sketchbook from my knapsack and drew a young woman kneeling beside the procession, her head bowed, her hands extended above her head, raising a bowl of rice in a devotional offering to the billows of fire-yellow-and-red cloth that whisked past her. I wanted my drawings to be personal keepsakes of our travels.

The next day, I woke early again, this time to meditate, with bedroom pillows for a cushion. The rain lashed down in sheets, and I used the sounds around me to open my awareness and ground me in time and place. I listened to trees rustling in the wind and to water pinging on the hotel roof and felt the damp air press against my open palms as I sat in open awareness for about thirty minutes.

When Victoria and the kids woke up, we ate breakfast and biked down a waterlogged, muddy road to the Mekong River, where we had planned to kayak for the day. As we approached the riverbank, we saw whole trees being swept away by the surging water. The waterway had morphed into fast-moving rapids of brown muck. It reminded me of our time in Sumatra, and I felt a hint of fear light up. Our guide thought it was safe to proceed, but a fellow traveler from Colorado, who I figured knew something about rivers, said, "He's out of his mind. I'd never send a kid out in that." The last thing I was going to do was place my trust in someone who couldn't see beyond his day's wages. I had learned my lesson from the Bukit Lawang rainforest, and I lectured my kids about safety first. As disappointed as they were, we came up with an alternative plan for the day. In the afternoon, as the kids enjoyed some downtime by the hotel pool, I unpacked my yoga mat, plugged in my earbuds, and moved to the poses as Nikki Wong called them out.

From Laos, we gritted our teeth and boarded a small Lao Airlines plane for a short flight to Siem Reap, Cambodia. What we experienced in that country was a surprise to all of us, heartbreaking because of its genocidal past and inspiring because we witnessed a young country desperately trying to grow and thrive.

When we arrived at our hotel, I convinced one of the workers at the hotel to sit for me so that I could draw her portrait. Chilly was a young woman in her twenties. She blushed and giggled when I stared at her face, trying to capture her expression.

Expressionist painters from Paul Gauguin to Gustav Klimt to Lucian Freud repeatedly tried to convey something of their sitters' inner lives. A figurative or portrait artist who is paying attention almost always conveys something of the model's personality and world, and I tried to do the same. But when I looked into her eyes to glean something of her inner self, I came up empty. Eyes don't give away hints of an inner glow; facial movements around the eyes betray a person's mood, and the viewer's brain is acutely aware of the meaning of infinitesimal expressions and tiny movements of micromuscles. It could read volumes into the slightest upturn of an eyebrow. While there was vastness in Chilly's facial expressions, there was nothing for me to learn from staring into her pupils. Yet like breath in meditation, eyes can serve as a focal point to let the surrounding meaning seep into consciousness.

I drew other subjects too. On the Mekong, I caught a glimpse of a man at the tiller of a boat that seemed gigantic for his comparatively slight frame. He was stationary and appeared to be stuck in invisible mud. There was something about how he and his giant boat just sat there in the stifling heat and placid water. I took out my sketchpad and a few pencils. I noticed, for the first time, subtle changes in the tones of gray and brown in that dead calm and the contrast in dimension between the small man and the acres of boat that he helmed. Not only was I beginning to see truly the way an artist sees, I also had a greater perception for the nuance of things.

In Bagan, Myanmar, Victoria and I met Khin Mar Lam, one of eight children of the owner of a vegetarian restaurant. The family worked hard to send some of the kids to university. But Khin Mar Lam stayed back to help. As I drew her portrait, she and her parents deftly avoided a Canadian lawyer at the next table who tried to engage them in a political discussion. He should have known that such conversations were bad for one's health in a country that, at the time, was ruled by military dictatorship.

The more I drew, the more meaning I derived from it and the more grateful I was to have learned that I was not by nature stuck with only whatever skills and intelligence were gifted to me at birth. All it took was being open to possibility, intention, and repeated practice. My drawing opened up a new dimension of travel for me. Spending an hour or so truly observing an image and perceiving the lines, edges, shadows, and perspectives was an unimaginable luxury. I then chose to turn those perceptions into drawings because I would add something of myself to the image, an expression that was personal and unique.

It was hard to say what our children absorbed from day to day in our travels in Southeast Asia, but they saw and heard it all and asked difficult questions. They saw some of the ugliness that war brings to civilians, and they saw extreme need. They could not help but be affected by it. When I asked Oliver what made the strongest impression on him, he said, "The poverty."

Our children had the opportunity to see their own country from the outside looking in. When they saw amputees and orphans in Cambodia, we talked about the millions of unexploded landmines, mortar shells, and bombs that were dangerous relics of the massive US incursions into that country. That was difficult, especially for Oliver, who was so used to seeing the United States as the winning team.

At a market in Myanmar, I asked Rita how she felt about the experience. She found it hard to say no to people who were hawking their wares, people she described as "less fortunate" than she. "They don't have as much food as me. I feel sad for them. Then I think about all I have. They're not starving, but . . . it's hard for me to look at." The scene of children selling in the market especially upset her. "Our guide said we shouldn't buy from them because those kids should be going to school."

In Vietnam, Victoria and I had an opportunity to teach our children about point of view in general and that any so-called unbiased information, like the sort one would expect from a museum, had an inherent perspective. Sometimes the point of view was overt, other times more subtle, but it was almost always present. Since the narrative of the war, as seen from the other side, was so different, it was an easy point to make. The experience reminded me of the first time I picked up a pencil to draw. To change perspective was to change perception.

When the five of us boarded a plane back to New York, the better part of two months had passed since we left Bali. We would still have a little time back in the States before I needed to return to work in September.

twenty-four

I t was mid-August when Victoria and I strolled along a dirt country lane in Putnam County, just north of New York City. The sun burned high, and the tall hemlocks threw mottled shadows. A woodpecker drummed against a nearby tree. As we ambled along at a Bali pace, a mosquito landed silently on my arm, and I felt its bite. I smacked it dead. "At least this one won't kill me." I was happy to be done with dengue fever, malaria, paratyphoid, and the monster's ball of bugs that carried tropical disease.

Victoria took my hand, and we interlaced our fingers. As we talked, I reminded her about a company retreat the following week, two weeks before I was set to return to work. "You're still on sabbatical," she said. "Once you get into a work mindset, it's all over."

We had spent so many intimate family moments together that separating was difficult for both of us. For me especially, balancing personal wants with business needs was a return to a familiar conflict.

"I know," I said, "but it's one thing not to attend an important meeting when I'm on the other side of the planet. It's quite another to skip it when I'm a car ride away. Especially after I've been away for so long."

Even sabbaticals were impermanent. Victoria kissed my hand and then looked over at me. "Imagine us having this conversation a year ago, before Bali."

I thought for a moment and then laughed. "We'd be arguing."

A few days later, a black Suburban SUV arrived at my home, and I set off for a nearly three-hour ride to the hotel at which the company was holding the retreat, a converted Victorian-style mansion in Watch Hill, Rhode Island. Perched on a bluff overlooking the ocean, the rambling structure and its vast grounds evoked old New England privilege. As we approached, I remembered the out-of-place feeling I had in Singapore and how far from Bali I was now.

I unpacked and took in the ocean view before I needed to head out to meet my partners. We had a full agenda of activities planned: a long hike, some physical team-building exercises, followed by massages, cocktails, and dinner. But first we had a discussion session. It was standard fare: airing any contentious issues, a discussion of our performance relative to our goals and how we might fill any gaps.

I left my room and met my partner Karl in the corridor heading to the meeting room. He wore sandals, I my flip-flops from Bali. My gait was much slower than his. He laughed. "Keep up, man!"

The dark wood paneling of the meeting room dampened the ocean sunlight streaming in from the windows. I saw my other partners for the first time since leaving for Bali.

"You back already?" Seymour asked. "Where'd the time go?"

Sabbatical, I realized, was an exercise in relativity. Our new experiences and the emotions attached to them created new memories and changed our characters. Time had passed slowly for me and my family. It was so thick and heavy we could nearly grip it. But for my professional colleagues who were engaged in the daily routines of work and home, their more linear stretch of time marched ahead briskly like soldiers on parade. Routine made their lives easier—they didn't have to think about or choose what to do next. Habit took over, hiding the passage of time and draining it from awareness.

I turned to one of the assistants, who brought me a box I had shipped from Bali. In it were desk ornaments I had commissioned from a Balinese artist. They were bronze bulls, reminiscent of both Bali's Hindu traditions and Wall Street's symbol of confident optimism. On the belly of each bull, hidden from obvious view, I had inscribed, "After Ten Years, Still Bullish." It had required a lot of planning and was meant to reassure myself and my partners that, despite my temporary departure, I was still sanguine about the firm's prospects. In a way, I returned the favor of Jordan's Leatherman multitool gift the December night before we bolted from the New York blizzard.

Reactions were muted. The partnership was eager to get on with business.

Over the next hour or two, I listened to updates on our investments and a review of the opportunities we were considering. I was interested in the subject matter but somehow could not connect. My mind, still stuck somewhere in a southern sea, was unable to shift quickly into business mode.

On the hike the next day, I chitchatted with various partners. Some expressed more interest in my experience than others. At one point I walked alongside Strauss, and we chatted about inconsequential things. I overheard one of my partners say, "Oh, good. Mom and Dad are talking."

When I returned home, we got down to the business of setting up for school and work. I packed away my shorts and T-shirts and pulled out my suits and button-down dress shirts. I stared at my collection of neckties and swallowed hard. I put my flip-flops in a closet and pulled out my polished brogues, the ones with the narrow toe box. I tried them on. They hurt when I tightened the laces. I tried a different pair, but those also pinched. It was as if my feet had expanded to fill the space I had created in Bali. I settled on a pair of simple black oxfords with thin leather soles.

"How are you feeling about galloping back into the fray?" Victoria said.

"Feels more like I'm about to sleepwalk my way back in." I knew the situation was charged, but I nonetheless hoped to change it.

She took my hand. "You're very lucky to have what you have, you know." I took a moment to appreciate that. And I saw the sense and opportunity in returning to the firm, even as I felt a nagging yearning for something new.

With a stab of chagrin, I realized I wasn't the only one experiencing reentry. "How about you?" I said. "What's next?"

She squeezed my hand and smiled. "The community center is doing fine without me."

"Thanks to you."

"And pretty soon, the kids will no longer need a full-time mommy. I want to go back to work, outside the nonprofit world this time." She'd given up a career to raise a family.

"And do what?"

"That's the thing. I'm going to look around for something."

∿

One Monday that September, after my morning meditation, I dressed in a pinstriped suit and trekked three miles from my downtown apartment to my office in Midtown. Having lived footloose for so long, I couldn't bear the claustrophobia of a crowded, sweltering, New York City subway. I committed to walking to and from work as long as the weather held.

Settling into my office, I reacquainted myself with my assistant. I had an out-of-place feeling that reminded me of when, decades earlier, I started a new job at a new company and could barely find the men's room.

After only a few weeks, I received a call from a headhunter asking me if I was interested in a CEO post they were trying to fill. I was gratified that sabbatical did not seem to diminish my prospects and asked for details. The company had a lot of elements that were attractive to me: it was public, a leader in its industry, and profitable. It had a healthy amount of cash and little debt. It was facing significant issues of transitioning from analog to digital media and had been challenged in its efforts to expand internationally. Both areas were strong suits for me.

I told the headhunter that I was interested so long as my firm could also invest in the company. There was no other way for me to both take the position and remain a partner in my firm. Nor was I ready to choose between the two. At the end of a series of interviews with the controlling shareholder, they said, "We want you, but we don't need or want any further investment in the company." If I wanted the position, I would have to leave the partnership. I wasn't ready for that. I was holding on. There had to be a way.

∿

I checked in with my doctor, Frieda Gu. My health stats that had been pushing into the uncomfortable zone before my sabbatical were back in normal range. Over the course of our time away, I had lost nearly twenty pounds, weighing in at a hair over one-sixty-two. My daily yoga practice had transformed my body; I was more lithe and flexible than I had ever been.

"How did you do it?" Frieda asked.

"Mostly, I paid attention."

I wasn't eating on the run, eating standing up, or breathlessly arriving late at a dinner table with thoughts about work still racing through my mind. I wasn't snacking while working on the next deal, product offering, or investor conference. I wasn't distracted by the smell of fresh pastry wafting into the street from a sidewalk café. Instead, I fully chewed my food. I noticed the tastes and smells of what I was eating. I sat with my family and ate home-cooked meals in an environment free of marketing messages encouraging me to be hungry for more.

I asked Dr. Gu to look into the pain in my left foot. She sent me for an X-ray and, when that showed nothing, an MRI. It turned out that walking to and from work wasn't the best idea I'd ever had. My feet didn't respond well to the pounding on New York's hard, unforgiving ground. The MRI showed a fracture in the left sesamoid, a small bone embedded in the tendon of the foot. Merging shoeless Bali and concrete New York was proving more difficult than I had imagined.

∿

One day, as autumn turned to winter, I arrived at my office in a foul mood. Freezing rain chopped through Midtown's canyons and wrecked the morning commute. My fingertips were red from the cold and my toes wet from a puddle I had stepped into.

I shook my umbrella dry and settled into my office chair. I was watching the rainwater sluice down the windowpane of my office and grumbling to myself about the city when I recalled a snippet of wisdom I'd picked up in Asia. I tapped my computer keyboard and pulled up a video lecture I'd seen by a French molecular geneticist turned photographer, author, and Buddhist monk named Mathieu Ricard. In a study on the connection between meditation and happiness, however that was measured, Ricard scored higher than any person previously observed. Researchers dubbed him the "happiest man in the world."

At my desk, I again listened to Ricard talk about one of his theories of the mind. Contrary to what some psychologists say about feeling multiple emotions simultaneously, Ricard believed that one emotion could crowd out another. "You cannot, with the same hand, both shake a man's hand and punch him in the face." Emotion could be deliberately chosen. He proposed that the antidote to sadness is an act of loving kindness. "If you're in a bad mood," he said, "go save a child's life."

I pressed the space bar on my computer to pause the video and reflected for a moment. Then in an act of utter grandiosity and self-interest, I opened a new tab in my Chrome browser and typed into the Google search box, "save a child's life." At the bottom of the screen was a group in Israel I'd not heard of called Save a Child's Heart, a medical charity that treated children with congenital heart disease from the Palestinian territories and underdeveloped countries around the world. An American pediatric cardiologist and surgeon, who later died while climbing the dormant volcanic cones of Mount Kilimanjaro, had founded it. While not small, the costs of treatment were a fraction of what they would be in the United States. I paused and took a moment to consider. With a few clicks on my keyboard, I entered my credit card information and made a commitment to help save a child's life.

I'd never done anything like that before. Perhaps as a result of compassion meditation practice, I was behaving more altruistically.

I recognized the hidden gift of Save a Child's Heart entering my world. Here was an unambiguous force for good in a part of the world that desperately needed it, a region where everything is nuanced and nothing is simple, where kindness among warring peoples is rare but possible. If our trip to Bali was a process of disengagement, just as I was now struggling to re-engage, Save a Child's Heart was an on-ramp to meaning that I could integrate into my life without having to forgo other ambitions. It was a ballast of compassion to counter the tilt of striving in a business career.

When I told the executive director what prompted me to make the initial donation, he asked, "Are you in a better mood?" I told him Ricard was right.

But I also wondered if I had become too, well, soft. Yoga, meditation, drawing, family, kids, charity. Maybe I needed to man up. While I didn't start eating raw meat for breakfast, at least not every day, I tried to recultivate a more aggressive business approach and reestablish my corporate machismo.

I continued to search for new investment opportunities. But in meetings, I felt that although I was in the room, I wasn't present. I felt I no longer belonged. That should have told me everything I needed to know. Over time, I again began to lose sleep and see some expansion in my waistline. I felt myself backsliding. My inner voice told me I'd forgotten all the wisdom I'd gained in Bali and simply jumped back into a situation that obviously was wrong for me. I had made the wrong choice.

∿

Then just before Thanksgiving, Strauss asked me to join him for a cup of coffee near Take-Two's office. We met at Balthazar, a French-styled bistro and a stalwart of the SoHo scene. It was late in the day, not quite dinnertime, and the restaurant had few customers. We took a small, round table. Strauss wasn't smiling.

"Here's the deal," he said and cleared his throat. "The guys don't think this is working."

Despite having been ready to have this discussion before I left for Bali, at this moment I found myself unprepared. I felt my pulse quicken as my amygdala triggered. I drew my attention to the emotion and breathed in to regain my sense of time, place, and balance. *Slow down. Create space.*

I asked for clarification. I knew the way the firm worked and that while consensus was important, the last word belonged to Strauss. "You've told me what the guys want," I said. "What do you want?" I pressed down with my big toe to feel the ground beneath me.

He paused. "I'd like to turn over another card." I didn't know what that meant, but I could see his discomfort, even distress. He said, "I'd like to think about it. I want you to do the same. We need to figure out a different sort of relationship."

He was trying to navigate through a delicate situation. I knew because I'd been on the other side of this conversation many times. When someone is ambivalent about being part of the organization, as I was, everybody knows it. Ambivalent people communicate their hesitancy in any number of verbal and nonverbal ways. It's impossible to fake intention.

We talked some more and said some very personal things to each other. Some were born out of anger, others of genuine affection. When we ran out of things to say, our waiter was nowhere to be seen, and an awkward silence settled over us like a sulfurous murk. I stood up. "I don't want to make this any more difficult than it already is. So I'm going to leave and let you pay for the coffee." He nodded. I walked out into the dark of that early November evening.

It was a fifteen-minute walk home. Rush-hour traffic had begun to build. Broadway was a river of headlights. Amid the honking horns and the roar of trucks and buses fighting for advantage before the next light turned red, I called Victoria. She knew that I was seeing Strauss and heard the tension in my voice. She asked, "Is everything okay?"

I raised my voice to be heard above the noise. "Sort of."

"Good news or bad news?"

I was surprised by my response. "A little bit of both." When I got home, Victoria and I talked for an hour.

After dinner with the kids, Rita asked, "Daddy, want to hear a song I wrote with Michael?" Michael was our children's music teacher whom Victoria credited with bringing music into our home and lives.

"Definitely."

She grabbed her guitar, sat on a chair in my bedroom, and sang a melodic riff:

When the weather's got you blue,
I'll always be standing next to you
In the pouring rain.
All you gotta do is call my name,
And I'll be there when you need me.
I'll take your hand; I'll show you the way.

When the sun doesn't look like it will rise,
I'll be there to dry your eyes.

When you want it all to end,
I'll teach you how to fight and defend.

I'll be there when you need me,
I'll take your hand,
I'll show you the way.

I'll stand by you tonight,
I'll hold you close and tight.
Let your tears fall
'Cause I'll be here forever and more.

Rita had developed instinctive empathic sense, and her timing could not have been better.

The next day I went to the Midtown office and started my morning by answering emails. I walked down the corridor to get some tea. When I passed by Strauss's office, he asked me to step in.

"I know what I want," he said.

"Good," I said. "I do too."

I had a fantasy of an arrangement that would keep me involved in a more passive role and protect my economic interests but grant me independence to pursue my own activities. It was my dream deal, and I thought it fit the realistic parameters of what could be agreed to. Remarkably, my model was close to what was on Strauss's mind.

In the days that followed, I retreated to the sanctuary of my yoga mat and meditation cushion. I returned to my barefoot practice in order to reground myself. My mind was far from the equanimity I sought to cultivate, but when I sat on my cushion or stood on my mat, I was immersed in an expansive calm. Having paid the premiums of a daily practice well in advance, I cashed in on my meditation insurance policy. I accepted the turbulence as transitory. Sometimes I even thought of it as a gift. I deliberately cultivated gratitude for my experiences. I focused on compassion for myself and my colleagues. In my mind, I forgave everyone, including myself, for having arrived at a place that never was anybody's intention. The path of forgiveness was powerful and led straight to the doorstep of serenity.

I realized that I was attached to my firm, had clung to it longer than I should have, and had succumbed to a stronger preference for avoiding losses rather than acquiring gains. It was a natural tendency, first described by economists Daniel Kahneman and Amos Tversky, called loss aversion. The fear of loss led to the rope burn of holding on for too long and too tightly to something that was inevitably slipping away. The balm was mostly in the conscious awareness of the phenomenon.

I thought about my conversation in Bali with Eric and the self-inquiry practice he'd suggested. At times, when my thoughts turned unconstructive, I heard his voice asking, "Is it true? Are you 100 percent certain that it's true?" And then I remembered his comment about making his life a sabbatical and thought that this was an opportunity to create that for myself.

When I called Eric to share my news, he said, "Congratulations!"

I was taken aback. "This doesn't feel like a congratulations moment."

"Oh, please. You engineered this entire situation. It was your choice."

What had transpired at work was the inevitable outcome of a decision I'd made to take a break, when I took the very first steps to embark on a new path. It was then that I'd made a choice and claimed responsibility for living fully. There were moments when I succumbed to rumination about the past and wondered if my sabbatical was a poor career choice because I was paying a price with my career. In those moments when I thought about what might have been, I reminded myself that taking the time to alter my circumstances was a deliberate expression of values that changed my family and me. I achieved an inner victory by gaining meaning in my life. My family understood the virtues of intention and courage. And I found love in the relationships with my wife and children. Besides, who knew what the future held? Life was long.

In the weeks that followed, as we negotiated the precise wording of a written agreement between the firm and me, I approached each of my partners. "All things change, and I'm okay with that." Rather than balling my hands into fists to fight like hell, as I would have done at an earlier time in my life, I exposed my palms in vulnerability—open heart, open mind.

When I reframed the situation in positive terms and emotions, the vector and tone of the conversation changed. What could have been ugly became amicable. Instead of fighting the force that was coming at me, I witnessed its momentum and flowed with it. I observed events as they transpired and responded instead of reacted.

∿

Victoria discovered that the professional world was not entirely welcoming to moms returning to the workforce after a long hiatus. She adopted an entrepreneurial approach and engaged in her own search for a special opportunity to crowbar her way back into the business world.

When I expressed concern about how we would manage it all, she quoted me back to myself: "Nothing is permanent. All things change. The trick is to lean into it and experience it fully." We fell into a new groove and struggled like everyone else to balance the demands of work and family. We found moments to reground ourselves, mostly through yoga, our family traditions, and quiet conversation in the same small home office in which Victoria hatched the original idea of our sabbatical.

The kids mostly slipped right back into their familiar patterns of friends, school, and activities. Just as they started school and with Victoria's help, they organized a book drive to help the school in Tanzania we'd visited.

Rita returned to her class a hero. Something about going to Bali made her special. In time, though, familiar social tensions reasserted themselves, and soon school became unbearable again. With our encouragement, she decided to switch schools permanently. We found one not quite like Green School but still progressive, creative, and nurturing. Replanted in more fertile soil, her shoot took root, and she blossomed.

Sam struggled to retain his sense of peace. In the face of the stress and competition in a Manhattan prep school, he periodically fell into bouts of silence at the dinner table just as he had before we left for Bali. He was a serious and competitive student who responded to the affirmation of good grades. But I found him more curious than he had been. When he expressed an interest in improving his Indonesian language skills, Victoria found an Indonesian graduate student to tutor him. Once weekly, they engaged in a Jewish-Muslim dialogue, in Indonesian, that enriched both of them. Throughout, Sam kept up with his Bali friends on Facebook and steadfastly refused to drink from plastic water bottles as if adhering to a religious prohibition.

He survived the college admissions process and was accepted to his first-choice school. When the admissions officer wrote to congratulate him, she added a handwritten note to the form letter: "I enjoyed reading about your trip to Bali and your continued interest in the Indonesian language." I laughed when I saw that and elbowed Sam. "You're welcome."

Nava too was taken with languages and embarked on her own online course to learn not Indonesian but Chinese. It was hard work, but we encouraged her to stick with it.

As Oliver entered high school, I noticed he was becoming a bit like Sam had been before we went on sabbatical. He began to take his schoolwork more seriously and studied hard for exams and quizzes that seemed to take place daily. I was concerned that the relentless pressure to perform was sucking the joy of learning out of him, just as it had for Sam, and that his desire to get into a good college and the work it involved would crowd out any other educational goal. His gang of buddies, for whom he yearned so intensely when we first left New York, was slipping away as friendships realigned in the transition to high school. Academic performance was becoming his sole focus, and other interests fell away along with his creativity. It distressed both Victoria and me. Before long, we encouraged him to join Rita, with whom he now argued only rarely, at her new school. He switched in his junior year. When Rita helped him clear out his locker, she found it stuffed with plastic bags.

"What's this?" she asked him.

"When I see kids throw out plastic bags, I collect them. I thought I'd send them to recycling. Eventually."

At his new school, Oliver again pursued his interests outside his schoolwork, and his general mood turned decidedly positive. He expressed an interest in playing the marimba, and Victoria found a man in Long Island who manufactured the instruments in Bali and imported them. When Oliver's arrived, it took a central place in our apartment. Once, when he was playing it, he paused and turned to me. "You know, I'm beginning to see it really was a big deal for us to take a sabbatical."

I took time to let the fractured bone in my foot heal and considered carefully the opportunities that came my way. Instead of saying yes to many of them, I was highly selective. Like the meditative wisdom that every wandering thought is an invitation to reorient, center, and restart, I decided to begin again.

At first, I mentored and coached CEOs as they built their companies for themselves and their investors. I was attracted to the creativity and energy of high-growth enterprises. I relied on my expertise and experience to help young technology companies grow. Periodically, in introductory meetings, my sabbatical story came up. It didn't connect with everyone, but with those it did, I developed a quick and easy bond that was deeper than usual. It was like a secret handshake with men and women who were curious and sought meaning beyond success and winning at all costs. When Steve Christian, the entrepreneur from Java, asked me to invest in a venture of his in Indonesia, I jumped at the chance. What excited me was not just the nature of the opportunity or the off-the-beaten path angle but the ability to be in business with creative people I liked and admired. And I wanted to keep a business toehold in Asia.

In the course of my mentoring, one of my people asked me if I would talk to a fellow entrepreneur who needed some guidance in an acute situation. The business was an online company that trained companies and individuals to excel in digital marketing. The co-owner told me that the relationship between her and the other primary owner had deteriorated to the point where they were suing each other. She had decided that the only way to protect what she had built was to put the company through bankruptcy. The company was a start-up that was just beginning to generate revenue, and Chapter 11 bankruptcy is rare in that world.

Victoria immediately came to mind. She had a background in marketing, technology, and start-up operations and was trying to stay involved in education after her time building the downtown school. She was looking for an entry point into business that would utilize her skills and not penalize her for the time away from the corporate world. This situation looked like an affordable entrée into a business that could leverage her skills and meet her interests. I ran it by her. She dug in, found out as much as she could about the company, and decided she wanted to be involved.

I went back to the entrepreneur. "We can play this one of two ways," I said. "I can advise you, which I'm happy to do, or I can bid for the asset because I think it's a pretty interesting opportunity. But I can't do both. You tell me which you'd prefer, and we'll do that."

"I'd like you to bid for it."

After weeks of due diligence, Victoria and I hired a lawyer to show up in a courtroom in San Francisco. We listened on speakerphone, me in our apartment, she in a taxi heading uptown for an appointment. The judge opened the auction. Two other bidders were in the room, one being the other shareholder. The bidding went a few rounds, and the gavel banged down. The judge declared the victor.

Victoria's cell connection was going in and out. "What did he say? Did we win?"

I said, "We won. It's yours."

Forgetting she was still on speaker in the courtroom, she let out a victorious yell. Muted laughter bubbled in from the other end.

Over the course of the next weeks and months, I did what I do—behaved like the CEO and, in her opinion, "mansplained" things to her. At first I was probably helpful in setting things up, mostly with the details around closing the sale, but soon she started straight-arming me out of the way. "Back off. I got this." I quickly learned to keep my mouth shut and offer advice only when she specifically asked for it. Other than that, my role was to listen without trying to tell her how to run things. She and the business were off and away. And just like that, Victoria entered one of the most creative and engaged phases of her career, devoting even more energy to the endeavor than she had to the community center.

As she got more and more into it, she wasn't always home to cook dinner for the kids and would ask me to deal with it, which I did. I also learned a lesson. The fact that I made dinner didn't mean I was taking responsibility for dinner. She still was the person who made sure there would be food in the house and dinner on the table every single day even if I was occasionally the one standing over the hot stove. The same applied to making sure someone walked the dog, dealing with the dry cleaners, shopping for the kids, and changing the bulbs. I had always understood this concept of responsibility in business but had never extrapolated it to the household or the family. It is an ongoing learning experience for Victoria and me as we test and evolve our traditional roles in the home.

I followed Julia Cameron's advice in her powerful book on creativity, *The Artist's Way*. I devoted two hours a week to go on an "artist date," time spent taking a solo expedition to explore something that interested me (I focused on the art galleries in Chelsea).

I also wrote "morning pages," three pages of stream of consciousness designed to clear the mind and chase away the self-critical voice that was so disruptive to creative flow. After a few sessions, I realized I wanted to add structure and direction to the exercise and write a book. This book. If others learned something from it, good. Besides, trying something new and creative, without regard to success or failure, would be applying directly the lessons I had learned on sabbatical.

As I engaged at work, my animal spirits stirred again. One day, I came across an opportunity that had all the markings of the original Take-Two situation. It was a large public company in the internet services sector that I thought was terribly managed. Investor sentiment was decidedly negative. Since its CEO had taken the helm eight years earlier, the stock price had collapsed over 80 percent. I dug in, analyzed the company, and developed a plan for change. I approached a board director whom I knew with a long-shot proposal.

"Here's the way I see it," I said. "If the company doesn't make a serious change now, the train will leave the station, and the enterprise will be unsalvageable. On the other hand, if the company acts now, I think the upside could be really exciting. I can turn this company around, create a vehicle for growth, and add a ton of value along the way."

I wasn't expecting a resounding reception. Boards of directors tend to be weary of outsiders with novel plans.

"That sounds like a breath of fresh air," he said. "Let me run it by a few other directors and get back to you."

Two weeks later, he called me back. "The thing is, the sitting CEO still has the board's confidence."

I felt my indignation rise. If management wanted to run the company into the ground, then the current CEO was the man for the job.

I wasn't about to give up. I called some hedge funds I knew and set up some meetings. We talked about possible courses of action. I was back in activist-shareholder land. Inevitably, proceeding would require waging an expensive fight, and any fight had the potential to turn nasty.

This time, I paused. This may have been a situation where a nasty fight was required, but did it have to be me to enter the battle? Did I really want to be hostile if I didn't need to be? Perhaps I would re-engage later in that sort of activity, but with my Bali experience so fresh, I knew the answer. I called the funds I had been talking to and dropped the matter.

Throughout that experience, I noticed that the character of my ambition and aggression had changed; it was no longer an overbearing imperative. My well-being did not depend on the next achievement. I realized that to compete, I needed to draw more on the wisdom of my experience than on the brute force of the mettle I'd developed in earlier years. The ethos of intention, presence, and creativity was as important to me as the culture of material success and accomplishment. Now when I needed to be tough in a business situation or negotiation, an appropriate aggression came naturally, though the edge had softened. I felt that I had become a better leader, entrepreneur, and executive. It was as if I had rewired myself into a certain kind of professional grace.

∿

As I went about my days, I strove to strike a balance of surrendering to what the world had to offer while fighting to tear opportunities from it. I sought to integrate the parts of me that wanted to engage, be effective, and compete with those parts that sought meaning, gratitude, and presence. I realized it was the intention to synthesize, not the synthesis itself, that motivated me. Like the peaceful warrior, my attempt to simultaneously engage and surrender would be ceaseless. The practices I'd cultivated in Bali, which by now had become routine, centered me.

I meditated daily, sometimes for three minutes, other times thirty and longer. I made yoga practice a near-daily part of my routine. When I got the call or message that business executives inevitably receive, the one that could ruin their entire day, I rolled with it better. When unhelpful thoughts conspired to commandeer my mind, as they still did periodically, their currents didn't carry me off. Instead, I stayed on the banks and watched them float past. I created space and recognized they were only thoughts that I didn't need to believe. By regularly taking time to fall back from fierce engagement, I had opened myself to a strength I had not previously known.

I found a studio in SoHo that, like Pranoto's, attracted artists to life drawing sessions. When I could afford the time, I drew to clear my mind, now in charcoal instead of graphite. Charcoal had depth, mood, and character that were absent in graphite, and it didn't leave a sheen on the page the way graphite did.

On Father's Day, Victoria's gift to me was a few sessions with a painting teacher who introduced me to oils. Alex Shundi was part painter, part chef, and part philosopher. And a gifted teacher. On weekends for about three hours, Alex and I talked about art history and painted on canvas. He followed my interests, wherever they led. At one session, we looked at early twentieth-century revolutionary art in Mexico; at the next, the meditative and impermanent art of Andy Goldsworthy; at a third, we spent ninety minutes discussing different hues of the color red.

In just the way drawing opened my eyes to line and edge, painting opened them to color. Color became vivid to me. I could see its complexity just walking down the street, my mind breaking down colors to their components, like factoring numbers. It was as if parts of my brain were lighting up for the first time.

I still found my own drawing and painting difficult but enjoyed the challenge and deep concentration the work required.

I recognized my inner critic and greeted it like a friend. When that inner voice peeped, I noticed it and deliberately shifted my thought pattern. I took a beat and reminded myself that almost any complex creative work looks wretched in its early stages. With enough practice and the proper intention, I knew my eye would get keener in its observations of light and edge and my hand would become truer in its production of image.

Still, meditation, yoga, and art were not a cure-all. One morning, I woke to a news story from Indonesia. Two of the Bali Nine had been sentenced to death and executed. Just when I was taking in the dawn of a new day, I felt as if a dagger had ripped through my heart. All the meditation practice in the world could not protect me from the anger and grief that I felt for men and families I had never met.

ᔕ

One day, I received a call from a professional friend who was a cofounder of one of China's most successful and, I thought, exciting technology companies. He pitched me on joining the company. "It doesn't get any bigger than this," he said. And the role he had in mind was a hand-in-glove fit with my interests and skills. More important, the company had a collaborative culture that openly promoted a positive optimistic outlook and a long-term orientation. Demanding without being threatening, patient without being foolish, it became successful, I concluded, not out of pure ambition but from an interest in exploring new areas and a willingness to try new approaches even if failure was a realistic possibility. It was the corporate version of Dweck's open mindset.

I thought long about the trade-offs and adjustments that I would have to make—working in another culture and language, the time and attention away from family because of travel demands, working in multiple time zones, and the general pressures of a fast-growing enterprise. It seemed as if I could be headed back into the situation I had left. Still, the opportunity to learn and grow while working with some extraordinarily smart and capable people appealed to me.

I equivocated about the decision, but in the end, it was Eric who convinced me to join. "Even Thoreau had to return to Boston." I realized that my quest would end like so many others, with a return home and a new sense of mission. Like the animal that had shed its skin, I was reborn. I accepted the offer and dove in with wholehearted intention. I even undertook to learn Chinese, again challenging myself to learn a difficult, even daunting skill.

Some of my earlier habits returned. I was traveling again, taking late phone calls, and missing dinners. But I realized that everyone needs to practice their trade. This is what I did. Yet I did it with a new perspective—more mindfully, as a meditation teacher would say—with less angst and stress, and always with an eye on where I was going. Not in conflict with my family but always looking to dovetail our endeavors and lives.

ᘜ

One steamy New York summer morning, on a day I was to board a flight for a business trip, Victoria and I attended a yoga class at the Kula Yoga Project on Warren Street. Kula was a low-key affair, situated on the third floor of a four-story walk-up and attended by dedicated yogis. Since we'd returned from Bali, I had gotten to know many of them in my daily practice. That day, Magi Pierce, an intelligent and talented instructor, led the way. As class got under way, I stood at the top of my mat in mountain pose with my arms by my side. I squeezed my shoulder blades together and turned my open palms to face forward. I felt my bare feet so solidly placed on the mat that they almost penetrated the ground beneath me. I settled into the pose and thought of that volcano in Java I'd climbed and imagined a different kind of mountain, one of soaring strength and dignity.

I transitioned into the down-dog position and felt my toes flex. I looked down and watched sweat descend in slow drops from my shirt and bead up on the mat below. I closed my eyes, took a deep breath, and again imagined myself back in Bali.

I let my mind wander and heard the sounds of Green School: students playing the marimba, irrigation sprinklers watering the student vegetable gardens, the serenade of the Ayung River rushing in the jungle ravine below campus, the background bird-song of the tropics. I imagined a puff of tropical breeze billowing through an open-air classroom, so real I felt it brush my face. I thought about my family's time in Bali, the ties and relationships Victoria and I developed with each other and our children, and the growth we experienced through shared emotion and experience. I thought about my effort to cultivate well-being through yoga, meditation, and art while engaging wholeheartedly in the world. It took time and intention for thoughts to change the brain and rewire neural pathways just as it took energy to synthesize the ethos of being and doing, but I was fully engaged in the effort.

Before I transitioned from the pose, I drew in another deep breath and opened my eyes. A small puddle, held by surface tension, rose from the mat. "Drop by drop," I recalled the meditation master's aphorism, "a cup is filled."

acknowledgments

N either this book nor the events described in it would
have been possible without my wife, Victoria, and her
extraordinary energy and vision. I am deeply grateful
for her love, friendship, and commitment to me and our family.
She is my inspiration, my true north.

Josh Getzler is a wonderful literary agent, and I would not
have written this book were it not for Josh's encouragement from
the moment the idea was hatched. That idea was as much his as
it was mine. I owe him the sense of accomplishment I feel for
having written it.

Sitting down to write started not with a pen but with a click
of a mouse, when I searched for a writing coach on the internet
and found Steve Adams, a talented writer and a patient and supportive tutor. Without him the task would have been too daunting and overwhelming to consider. Ours was a cyberrelationship;
we never met in person. But our emails and biweekly phone calls
kept me on track. Thank you, Steve.

Where Steve left off, Peter Gelfan continued. Peter is a gifted
editor. I balked when, after reading the first draft, he told me
that the book needed to be completely rewritten. But eventually
I did rewrite it with his suggestions in mind. The work product
was vastly improved. He stuck with the project through thick

and thin, and I am very thankful for his counsel, dedication, and skill with which he applies his craft.

Thank you also to Mark Fretz, Scott Waxman, and the team at Radius Book Group. Without their constant vigilance and competent management, this book would not have seen the light of day. And thank you to Sandi Mendelson, David Kass, Fauzia Burke, and the teams that have worked tirelessly to promote the book and to make sure it got into the hands of a readership I value dearly.

Finally and certainly not least, thank you to my family, friends, and many colleagues, especially at Young Presidents Organization, who read and reread the manuscript and provided valuable feedback, patience, and support.